Ethical Hacking

A Beginner's Guide to Cybersecurity, Penetration Testing, Network Defense and Information Security Risk Assessment

Ethan Caldwell

ISBN: 9781807655389

Published by TPSA Publishing

Table of Contents

Introduction

Let's think back to a little over 10 years ago. The whole field of IT security was basically unknown. Back in the '90s, there were barely any professionals who could say they worked in "cybersecurity" and there were even less of those that actually knew what the area was about to become.

Security was essentially just anti-virus software. You know, that annoying popup which screams at you every time you try to get a file off the Internet. Sure, packet filtering routers and similar technologies were also popular, but it wasn't really seen as, well, important in the slightest.

The concept of a hacker at the time was more akin to the hacker memes we have today. It came mostly from movies that Hollywood made...or just referred to someone that got a low score while playing golf.

It was ignored. Nobody really saw hacking as much of a threat. After all, what was there to gain at the time? It was seen as mostly an annoying triviality that might pop up every now and again. Today, we understand it is a massive threat that can impact multi-billion dollar corporations and even our governments.

It was ignored, and at the time, it was obvious why. Unfortunately, later on the whole IT industry would feel the impact that hackers can leave. These days, the number of IT system security professionals is over 61 thousand around the world. This isn't for no reason. In fact, the field of cybersecurity is not only growing, but growing at a faster pace than the already-growing tech industry according to the ISC. There are now more security companies out there than anyone really cares to remember and trust me, most of them do work that's much more important than a mere antivirus.

Cybersecurity has even seeped into the mainstream, with countless people authorizing things through their firewalls and using VPN's every day to watch videos unavailable in their location.

There are so many ways to address any security problems that it can be a true headache to think about it. Heck, even just considering the alternatives of a single program is enough to give you a migraine from the sheer amount of competition out there.

Since the 90's, the world has changed massively. I mean, think about the last day you spent without using an electronic device. Chances are you don't even remember that. So, what does all this change carry for your home? For your computer? Does it mean you're thrust into a dangerous world every time your computer, phone, or any other smart device is as much as turned on? Well, that's pretty much what it means, as every single one of those changes led to the world and the criminals in it changing to meet the new surroundings, too. In the digital world, you will find a playground which is padded with mines that need but one single touch to explode, if they even need that much. Even the simplest of things can spell quite a bit of trouble for you.

If you ever plug into the internet without a decent firewall, there is a certain chance that your system will get hacked in mere minutes.

Whenever you open an unassuming email from friends or family, there is always that chance that the email will open a backdoor to your system. This means that it will take a hacker very little time to gain access to even the most private parts of your computer.

If you use your Internet Messaging program to download and execute a file, you should not be surprised if your desktop turns into a virus hot zone.

Even when you are browsing through trusted websites, you are completely open to hacker attacks. When this happens, your sensitive files are at risk of being taken or deleted. Sadly, the fear of being a target of an online drive-by is often more than a fear and you can be targeted completely out of the blue. It is not a rare occurrence.

More often than not, people like to spread the word on the dangers of cyber-terrorism. The fear, uncertainty, and doubt that people generally feel when it comes to this subject are, however, anything but unjustified. People are often blind to how high the chance of a digital cataclysm actually is. Organized crime and terrorism have their finger everywhere, and this includes the digital world, too. Several organized terrorist cells are often raided. When their computers are found, the majority of what's on them is cyber-hacking plans and similar files that depict how they would attack the infrastructure of the United States.

You might remember August 14, 2003. This was the day when the biggest power outage in the history of the United States happened. Around 20 percent of the U.S. population was left without power for more than 12 hours. It is very easy to make yourself believe the most light-hearted narrative and say that some trees fell or strong winds damaged some part of the network. While this explanation might be correct, think about this: 3 days before the power outage, the Microsoft Blaster worm was unleashed on the Internet. This worm is known to be one of the most dangerous and volatile worms ever made. While this might have been a coincidence, one can not help but be just a tiny bit skeptical.

You might be thinking that all of the fear and heaviness caused by cyber-terrorism is not justified. You might think that since nothing happened so far, nothing will. But think about this: nobody expected 9-11 to happen. Everybody knew that there was a safety risk when it comes to airport security and terrorism, yet nothing was done about it.

The skepticism is understandable and welcome, as some skepticism is never a bad thing. But you should trust me when I say that cyber-terrorism is a very dangerous yet likely thing. You should trust the media when they start panicking about small cyber-attacks because that's how it all starts.

You should be careful when it comes to this. A hacker is like a burglar. They try to poke away at your safety until they can pin-point a place from where they can enter your safe space and take your valuables. Every second of the day there are hacker groups and organized criminals that are digging away at your safety. You should never let them succeed. Nobody should ever sit back and watch another person take what they hold dear and desecrate their safe space. Help yourself by learning more about this, and use the resources that are available to you in order to protect yourself as much as possible.

While increasing your security might seem like something straight out of movies, I assure you that it is something that you can do quite easily. It's more about what you think than anything else. You can compare it to working out or studying. As long as you are adamant and have a schedule on which you do certain things, it will quickly become a part of your life. If you don't integrate it into your day-to-day schedule, you will quickly start to forget it and find excuses not to do it. Security is a process and not a goal. So, it's important for you to make it a part of your routine and soon enough, you are going to be able to do it without thinking about it.

If you avoid this, however, you will be hit sooner or later. The best thing that you can do for yourself now is to educate yourself and get some knowledge on the subject. You can't protect yourself from something you do not understand, and protect yourself from it you must. It is not your right to protect yourself, but your duty. Getting to know something that might be dangerous for you is the best thing you can do to keep yourself safe. If you fill the gaps in your knowledge, you will be able to prepare yourself for most things.

What is well known and plain to see is that you are going to have to always keep track of it in order to protect yourself from malicious users everywhere. This is where the know-how in this book comes in and saves the day. It will give you a way to implement the technology available to us currently and the knowledge that has been accumulated over the years to keep your systems secure for a while. Keeping your system safe is impossible unless you get into the mind of the malicious user and use the knowledge that you obtain while doing so. See which tools they use and use the same tools to see the weaknesses in your system that they could see if they were targeting you. Unless you do this, any other assessment of how secure your system is can be very inaccurate.

Ethical hacking encompasses many different legal and safe activities. It is necessary to improve systems all across the globe and make them safer. The activities include, but are not limited to, white-hatacking, vulnerability testing, and penetration testing. While the benefits of this kind of activity are relatively hard to see, if you look into it a bit more, it becomes clear as day. The only way to improve and keep up with the changing times is to improve yourself. This is done by testing your system and improving upon the results that you get from the testing. The book mainly covers what it means to be an ethical hacker and how you are supposed to do this correctly in order to find effective countermeasures and close any back doors that your system might have in order to keep malicious hackers out of it.

Who is This Book For?

First of all, it is important to emphasize the fact that should you choose to use the knowledge provided by this book for malicious activities on your own, the blame is all on you. No one else who was associated with you gaining the knowledge is not to blame, nor are they liable for the way that you use the knowledge. The contents of this book can be used by white hat hackers (ethical hackers) and black hat hackers (crackers) alike. The book gives such a close look into the cracker mentality that it becomes a good source of study for crackers themselves. The methodologies in the book can be used both ways. The responsibility of using the knowledge correctly falls on you completely. You should always use it in authorized ways.

To be an ethical hacker means to focus your efforts on detecting security holes that might have been overlooked and find ways to fill up those holes. Whichever kind of testing you run on your system will help you out to manage and improve your system, as well as any other system you might do this for. Computer security is nothing to scoff at. It is an issue that should always be taken seriously.

The same can be said if you are doing this for another individual. Your aim is to protect their system from malicious users and plug in the holes which seem to be the most problematic. If you read this book correctly and soak up all of the knowledge, you will always be on your A-game when it comes to computer security. You will enjoy the feeling of being self-sufficient in that regard and will also bask in the glory of being a helpful individual to anyone that has concerns with computer safety. No matter what kind of system we are talking about and how far advanced that system is, there are always going to be hundreds if not thousands of possible ways to crack it.

This book will help you understand the following:

- The results of several important and impactful case studies made by several different experts on the subject

- Different hack attacks that are widely used in the cracking community and all of the nuances that lie beneath

- The countermeasures that you can take to protect yourself

In order to be prepared for the tasks yet to come and be able to properly hack your systems, you should get to know the info in Part 1 of the book. There is an old adage that says: "If you fail to plan, you plan to fail." This is very true about hacking, especially when it comes to the ethical part of it. There are several steps you need to take before you can start working. You need to get permission from the owner of the system first and develop a general game plan on how you are going to approach it. Some may look at the information in this book and say that it is made to turn script kiddies, people who use automated tools to crack into systems with little to no technical knowledge, into actual hackers. This, however, is wrong. The knowledge presented in this book is provided to you for ethical purposes. You are supposed to use it to hack your own systems or the systems you have permission to hack in order to make the system itself more secure and the information on the system safer.

There are some chapters you can skip in this book. For example, if you are not using a Windows operating system, then there is no point in reading the chapters that detail how to use them.

The book goes into the explanation assuming a few things:

- You have an average grasp on concepts and terms that are related to information, computer, and network security
- You can differentiate ethical hackers from crackers
- You have a computer and a network that you can apply these techniques to
- You can access the Internet and get the tools that might be necessary for some of the jobs
- The owner of the system gave you permission to use the methods and techniques from the book.

The book is divided into seven parts. You should get well-acquainted with the format, as you might need to jump around from one part to another. Each of these chapters gives you different methods and techniques that will help improve your ethical hacking skills.

The Difference Between Ethical Hacking and Cracking

For a long time, there has been a great deal of controversy regarding the term "hacker". The general populace automatically assumes that a hacker is someone who does the line of work in an unethical way and aims to hack into systems for their own gain. This, however, was not always the case.

Before hacking became a wide-spread criminal activity, the word "hacker" had a very positive meaning. It was used for the best of the best when it comes to programming. The likes of Linus Torvalds were proclaimed to be hackers. This image of the word changed very quickly when outbreaks of cybercrime started happening. The media took it upon themselves to clear up the happenings while muddying the names of the finest programmers at the time. The programming community was outraged at this and many fiery debates started erupting over the subject. Many influential names from both of the communities rose up to give their input. But, alas, it was all for nothing. The narrative that the media pushed was already widely accepted by the public and it was too late to change it. The word "hacking" was labeled as a negative one. This was not helped by the cracking community enforcing the narrative that hacking is strictly a malicious activity. The people in the cracking community like to carry the title of "hacker" with great pride. This is seen as an insult by the programming community, as a hacker should be a title only given to those that have shown great expertise when it comes to programming.

There are several parallels that need to be drawn in the discussion. While the cracker subculture is a part of the programming community, the programming community aims to stifle and denounce any efforts made by the cracker subculture. This is where the term "cracker" came from. The programming community sees crackers as the most dangerous and heinous individuals. In order to prevent as many people as possible from using the term "hacker" for these individuals, they took it upon themselves to find a new term to replace that one in the narrative. This is where the term "cracker" comes into play. Once the term was coined and generally accepted by programmers, it was immediately pushed into the media. Great efforts were made to clear up the difference. While it, at first, appeared as it was going somewhere and that some change was on the horizon, in the end, it fell into the water. The media was adamant on pushing their narrative and, on top of that, people from the cracking community started calling themselves hackers.

Programmers generally use this differentiation and call malicious hackers crackers. Some people outside of the community stick to it too, but the majority of the public was already influenced to the point where the damage is irreversible. Still, it is important to make the differentiation. It is imperative that we never forget about it, as there are great names such as the aforementioned Linus Torvalds whose names are always connected to the term "hacker".

What you should keep in mind is that hacking is like any other trade. A parallel is always drawn between it and locksmithing. Why? Because the main principles of the two are fairly similar. Hackers try to find weaknesses in the system, but this is legal if it is done with good intentions and the permission of the owner of the system. The act of lock-picking is considered highly illegal and is a crime of its own, but a lock-smith needs to do it from time to time in order to satisfy their clients' needs. Imagine being stuck outside of your own house and leaving the keys on the inside. You don't really want to break down the door or damage your windows, so you call a locksmith to help you break into your own home, as funny as it may sound. Hacking works on a similar principle. While the act itself can be illegal, you will always want the help of an experienced hacker when you are working on improving the security of your system.

It is a fact that hackers, white hat hackers to be precise, are necessary for the industry today. Many corporations and organizations offer classes and payrolls for skilled hackers. Why? A computer system is like an organism. You build up immunity by getting sick. The situation is similar with computer systems. The only way to really improve your security is to suffer an attack. A weakness becomes very apparent once somebody abuses it. Today, many companies hire skilled hackers in order to improve the security of their systems. Most hacking attacks happen in a pattern. If you perform an attack on your system and adjust your system to be able to prevent such an attack in the future, it will be able to prevent all of the attacks of the same kind or at least slow them down. However, only the most skilled are hired for these jobs. You would not want an inept doctor treating your illnesses.

Hence, you don't want an inept hacker to fiddle around with the delicates of your system. The individuals who do this line of work are usually deemed to be hackers by the whole of the programming community. This is the most respectable thing you can do with your hacking skills, as it takes a great deal of expertise and it is done for a good cause.

When we are talking about the different kinds of hackers it is important to point out that there are categories based on the legality and legitimacy of their activities, rather than the level of skill they possess. Based on this, we have the following categories:

White hats - White hat hackers are hackers that good-intentioned programmers want to be. They work to keep systems safe. They find weaknesses in the system and find ways to remove them. The line of work white hats have is usually very well paid and they are considered to be one of the most valuable technology assets. The work done by white hat hackers is not illegal. White hat hackers have the permission of the owner when they start working on a system.

Black hats - Black hat hackers are your typical crackers. Their work is usually fueled by malicious intentions and selfishness. They work to crack a system in order to find data that they or someone else might want. This is considered to be highly illegal and is the reason that the word "hacker" has such negative connotations. They do the same thing as white hats, but out of malicious reasons and without the permission of the owner. There is a sub-group of black hats called script kiddies. No one in the community likes script kiddies, not even black hats themselves. Why? Because script kiddies have almost no skills in the line of work and use pre-scripted tools to do all of the work.

Grey hats - Grey hat hackers fall somewhere in the middle of the spectrum. Their activities are illegal, but they do not steal or destroy the data, rather they do it for sport. They usually contact the owner of the system they cracked in order to offer them a fix for the vulnerability.

The Hacker Ethic

There are two rules that make the difference between crackers and actual hackers. The two rules were made regarding the legality and legitimacy of the hacking process. They are the following:

Information-sharing is good for everyone. Every hacker has the duty to share their knowledge. They do this by writing open-source code and helping people to improve their systems as much as possible.

Using one's knowledge in order to crack systems for fun and practice is alright as long as no illegal activities are done through this activity.

These principles are widely employed, but not by everybody. Most hackers work under the first ethic by writing open-source software. This is taken a step further by some more extreme individuals that believe that all information should be available to everyone. The GNU project stands behind this philosophy and believes that any kind of control over information should be considered bad.

The second ethic is usually considered to be a tad more controversial, as there are individuals who consider that any kind of cracking should be considered immoral and illegal. What separates grey hats from black hats is the fact that they do not use their expertise to destroy or steal information. This is why they are considered somewhat benign in the community. There are several rules of courtesy among hackers. Once a grey hat hacker cracks into someone's system, he should always contact the owner of the system itself in order to tell them how the attack was made and how the system can be protected from similar attacks.

Almost all hackers are willing to share their knowledge and expertise on the subject. This is the most reliable way that the two ethics manifest. There are huge networks that work as places where the community can gather and where individuals can exchange experiences and tools, as well as techniques and tips.

CHAPTER 1: WHAT IS ETHICAL HACKING?

Cyber criminals present one of the biggest problems somebody can find in the digital worlds. There was a time when hackers weren't taken as seriously, but things changed drastically in the past several years. In India, for example, there are many companies that pay hefty sums of money to hackers in order to protect some of their sensitive and valuable information. It was reported back in 2013 that 4 billion dollars were lost by Indian companies during that year alone due to cyber attacks.

As the world of business evolves and becomes more and more technologically dependent, many companies were forced to enter the digital ecosystem and adopt the technologies that the ecosystem offers in order to function more efficiently. The need for more efficient ways to protect information is becoming more and more prominent due to the threat of more and more intense and damaging breaches of security. All of these changes made the shortage of talented people in the information security sector apparent.

Nasscom reported that the need for white hats far surpassed the number of white hats they had in 2015. There were 15,000 certified ethical hackers in India, versus the 77,000 that were actually needed.

What is Ethical Hacking?

Ethical hacking is the practice of using hacking techniques in order to help out systems with protecting the important information stored on it. This is a new league in the IT-sphere of programming which is gaining more and more recognition. This line of work employs people in order to hack into security systems and locate weak points in them and find a way to fix them.

The techniques employed by white hats and black hats are very similar and usually the same. The difference is that white hats need to make improvements to these techniques in order to stay on top of the more malicious counterparts in the line of work. Corporations that use security systems and work with huge amounts of sensitive information hire white hat hackers in order to prevent malicious individuals from accessing the information stored on the system. A white hat hacker's job is to hack into the system of the employer in order to locate the parts of the system that are at risk and fix the holes. The first step that every white hat takes is called penetration testing. This is a way to find vulnerabilities in systems. It is an easy way to assess the strength of the system.

Ethical hacking includes many services. Some of these are:

- Application Testing: Detects the flaws in a system
- Remote or war dialing: Tests modem connections
- Local network testing: Works to analyze the work of protocols and devices in the system.
- Wireless security: Checks the overall security of the entire framework.
- System hardening: Strengthens the system and fixes the holes in the system
- Stolen laptop: This is done through the PC of an employee that has access to a bit of information. It checks the personal information stored in software.
- Social engineering: Uses the personality of the hacker to gain access to a system.

The Need for Ethical Hackers

As I have mentioned a few times, cybercrime is becoming more and more of a big deal. Crackers are becoming more and more sophisticated. They also gain access to more and more funding due to the many malicious organizations that want to steal information from important sources.

Every day, businesses need to improve their own systems in order to get with the advancements in hacking tactics and techniques. Hackers find hidden vulnerabilities in computers more and more often, so in order to protect your system, you will always have to improve your security. This is the same for every corporation that handles very sensitive information. White hats are usually well-trained professionals who work towards improving these systems.

Some traditional companies have a problem when it comes to the understanding of white hat hacking. The banks in India have often faced vicious hacking attacks that cost them a great deal of money. Their lack of faith in the benefits of ethical hacking led to their defenses against cybercrime being quite minuscule.

There is a malware called "darkhotel" which hit hotels and several other parts of the industry. This proved that the industry was falling behind when it comes to cybersecurity. The malware itself was used to gather information on people of interest that reside within the hotels by using the hotel's Wireless Network access.

The cracking community constantly grows when it comes to tools and techniques. New kinds of malware, worms, and viruses are made every single day. Due to this, businesses are becoming more aware of the benefits of ethical hacking and how it can help protect their networks.

The bottom line is that owning an enterprise in this day and age is as risky as it could be due to the number of malicious users that have access to so many different tools. This is why every system should be tested on a regular basis in order to keep up with the times. There is a holistic approach that is involved in the assessment of a system due to the complexity of the field of computer and network security. There are many interactions and operations that are involved in any security system and some of them might be very fragile. Ethical hackers are the best people to do this. They are individuals with the ability and know-how that can help anyone fine-tune their system.

How is Ethical Hacking Different from Cracking?

As I have stated a few times, the techniques that all hackers use are similar, if not the same. The tools and techniques used are universally accepted by all of the people that involve themselves in this activity. The only difference between ethical hackers and others is why they are doing what they are doing. Crackers, or black hats, are fueled by their own selfish and malicious reasons like profit or harassment. The efforts of white hats are made in order to prevent the black hats from taking advantage of systems.

There are several other things that can help you differentiate black hats from white hats:

The goal of the activity: While it is true that white hats use all of the techniques that have been developed by black hats, they do this in order to help out an individual or corporation. This is done in order to determine how a black hat would approach the system in order to spot flaws and help fix them.

Legality: The main differentiation between ethical hackers and crackers is the fact that, even though they do the same thing in the same way, only one side is legally acceptable. White hats have the consent of the system's owner before doing it, while black hats break the law by doing it without the owner's knowledge.

Ownership: White hats are hired by different companies to help them out with improving their systems. Black hats do not hold ownership over the system and they are not employed by somebody who does.

Roles and Responsibilities of an Ethical Hacker

The ethical side of hacking is no simple thing. While white hats are often regarded highly in the programming community, as well as among business owners, they are still regarded as criminals by many. The very activity is considered to be immoral by many. Many white hats prefer not to have the connotation of "hacker" next to their name due to the reactions they may get.

In order to keep their practices legal and prevent others from viewing them as criminals, white hat hackers need to be well acquainted with their responsibilities and stick to the guidelines. The following rules are some of the most important for white hat hackers:

- An ethical hacker is always supposed to ask for the consent of the owner of the system before starting to get into it. You will need the approval of the owner for every activity that you do on the system and you are expected to provide the information you gained through your activities to the owner.

- Once the hacker analyzes the system, he must make his findings and plan known to the owner before taking action.

- The hacker must notify the owner of what was found during the search.

- The hacker is expected to keep his findings and activities confidential. Due to the nature of ethical hacking which is helping the security of a system, the hacker should not disclose the information to anyone else.

- Remove all of the found vulnerabilities after finding them in order to stop black hats from entering the system without authorization.

In order to be successful in the line of work, you are going to need a certain set of skills. The knowledge a white hat hacker needs to possess is both wide and deep. It needs to encompass several parts of the computer technology field and needs to be highly detailed. Some of the skills that are needed are:

- Detailed knowledge of programming - Any professional that works in the fields of Software Development Life Cycle and application security is required to possess this knowledge.

- Scripting knowledge - This kind of knowledge is important to anyone who works on host-based attacks and network-based attacks.

- Networking skills - Most threats to the system come from networks. Due to this, you will need to know about all of the devices that are connected to the network and how they interact with it.

- Knowledge about different platforms used on different kinds of devices

- Knowledge on how to use hacking tools and techniques available on the market

- **Knowledge on servers and search engines**

CHAPTER 2: HACKING AS A CAREER

It is safe to say that identifying yourself as a hacker will make a few heads turn and give you some unpleasant stares, as people who do not know the difference between black hats and white hats will immediately assume that what you are doing is highly illegal. No matter what you are doing, whether it's helping out a branch of the military in order to improve the security of the classified information, or hacking into a school's database in order to see what loopholes can be abused by unauthorized users in order to gain access to the data, your efforts will usually be frowned upon to a certain extent by others. People will usually assume that you work as a part of an underground society of vandals and consider it not to be a valid career choice.

This is everything but true. Hacking can make a career unlike any other. In order to properly work as a certified ethical hacker, you are going to have to go through a bunch of prep work and training. A diploma or certificate regarding computer security is not always required, but it is always nice to have. What you will need is extensive knowledge of the subject. Knowing how computers work and interact with one another is the most important part when you are looking to get into the line of work. A lot of movies and TV shows like to show hacking to be something glamorous. They never show everything that goes into the line of work. Experience and knowledge are big deals when it comes to hacking, which is sometimes easily overlooked.

With that in consideration, if you did all of the learning on your own by using your systems, this line of work can be more challenging than it might have appeared to be at first.

If you had practiced using your own equipment, the next logical step is freelancing, where you can get some more experience and some endorsement for your activities. As you may expect, however, hacker freelancing isn't exactly the most stable position ever, so you might experience some serious lows when it comes to finances. It is a great way to gain more experience and some cash on the side. It is also a great way to build up an impressive resume. Freelancing is usually a great place to start.

After you have gained a substantial amount of experience, you should start sending job applications to tech companies to see if your experience is needed. You can send applications to many big firms. This is smart, as they tend to pay more for these services. However, there are many smaller companies which will be more eager to hire you, and are ready to pay a bit more for your services if you are good enough. Always keep your sights open, as you can find work in this industry if you have the skills.

Being an ethical hacker is quite a challenging line of work due to the fact that a proper white-hatacker needs to know everything about systems and networks. This is why certain organizations started to give out certifications that support talented hackers when it comes to work. Aspiring ethical hackers have been looking into getting these kinds of certifications as proof of skill. There are several certifications that give some big benefits. Some of these benefits are:

- Hackers with these certifications have the necessary knowledge to build and maintain security systems. If you prove to be good at this field of work you will be a great asset to any organization that might look to hire you.
- Hackers with these certifications have an increased chance to get higher salaries. A certified ethical hacker can hope for a salary of $90,000.
- It validates your efforts and makes it easier for you to get a job in companies and makes you more noticeable among your peers.
- Most organizations prefer certified individuals when it comes to system security due to the growing needs of the field.
- Startup companies look for certified individuals. These companies pay quite a penny for individuals that do these jobs.

The Different Kinds of Ethical Hacking

When it comes to ethical hacking, there are several kinds of practices that are employed. Due to the outstanding variety of possible cyber attacks, every company wants to test as many possibilities as possible. This is why they employ individuals with different degrees of knowledge. These are the so-called boxes. There are three kinds.

Black Box Ethical Hacking

Black box ethical hackers know nothing about the organization whose systems they are trying to get into. These people do not have a focus on a particular part of the system or a particular method. They use all of the tools at their disposal in order to crack the system. The attacker has no focus due to the fact that he has no information on the organization he is attacking.

White Box Ethical Hacking

White box ethical hackers are concerned with how much time and money will go into a job. When a white box ethical hacker starts working on a system, they know everything about the organization. They are used to emulate an attack that could be executed by someone close to the company or inside of the company. These attacks target the specific parts of the system in order to strengthen them. The drawback of this method is the fact that the hacker will attack the already known vulnerabilities and possibly overlook other vulnerabilities.

White box ethical hackers usually cooperate with teams of different people from Human Resources, Upper Management, and Technical Support Management.

Grey Box Ethical Hacking

Gray box hacking is somewhere between the previous two. It combines the two attacks. It has a certain amount of information on the company, but that information might change from time to time. It has the same drawback of white box ethical hacking due to the obvious vulnerabilities.

The History of White Hat Hacking

Ethical hacking is not a thing of the new age. It has been around for a long time under different names. The first documented instance of ethical hacking happened when the United States Air Force executed what they called a "security evaluation" of their systems. The Multics operating system was tested in order to see if it could be used to store top-secret files and documents. During this test, it was determined that Multics is better than the other options that were available to them, but it was still lacking and had many vulnerabilities when it comes to security which could be exploited with not much effort on the side of the cracker. The test was made to be as realistic as possible as they believed that this is the only way to get precise results that can be considered proof. The tests varied from simple information gathering to full-on attacks that endangered the entire systems. Ever since then, there have been a few more reports of the US military doing these kinds of activities.

Until 1981, white hat hacking was not known as a term to many people, but it was then that The New York Times introduced the term and labeled it to be a positive kind of hacking tradition. There was an employee in the National CSS that wrote a password cracker software. When he decided to disclose this software he was met with great outrage. The company was not angry at the existence of the software, but at the fact that he kept the existence of the software hidden. In the letter of reprimand the NCSS stated that the company sees the fact that employees finding security weaknesses as beneficial to the company and that the company encourages it.

Dun Farmer and Wietse Venma were the first to see the potential of white hat hacking. They were the people who turned it into a technique that can be used to assess the security of a system and improve it later on. They pointed out that, after a certain time, once they have gathered a certain amount of information, they could crack into a system and deal a great amount of damage to it should they choose to do so. When they talked about what can be done through white-hat hacking, they gave several examples about how information can be gathered and exploited, and how, using this knowledge, attacks can be prevented. They made an application from all of the tools that they used during their research and made it available for download to anyone who might be interested. The program is called the Security Administrator Tool for Analyzing Networks, also known as SATAN. The program saw a great deal of attention from the media in 1992.

CHAPTER 3: MAKING MONEY FREELANCE

Ethical hacking is a huge field. The amount of jobs available is huge, which leads to them paying more and more as time goes on, as there aren't enough ethical hackers in order to cover all of these positions at all times.

In my opinion, the best way to earn money with ethical hacking is by going freelance. In this chapter, we'll be going over the pros and cons of doing freelance work, as well as how well you can expect to earn, and the process of becoming a freelancer.

What Is Freelancing?

Freelancing is basically becoming a company yourself. While you don't have to set yourself up as a CEO or anything, it does serve to paint a good picture. A freelancer is basically a one person company. You'll need to be your own marketing, your own PR, your own accountant, and your own employee. This takes a lot of grit, so if you're someone that's satisfied with a regular, 9-5 job, then I'd advise against going the freelance route. On the other hand, if you're someone that wants to try very hard, get to the top of the field, and rake in ludicrous amounts of money, then this area is for you.

Freelancing basically means abandoning the traditional concept of employment and becoming something of a full-time contractor. You'll need to pick your own clients, as well as find them yourself. This can be quite difficult for beginners, though we have a few great ways listed out below.

As a freelancer, you can also dictate your own hours, which is great. If you're an early riser, then you can start work at dawn, but if you're a late owl, nobody will judge you for starting your work day at 4AM. This also means you don't have to do all your work at once, and can segment your work so that you only work for the time that you're actually productive.

You'll also only get paid for the stuff you do, so make sure to reflect this in your hourly rate. It's not uncommon for freelancers that are in an area that usually pays $20 an hour to command $30 an hour or higher rates. Freelancers are also usually considered to be more competent than in-house employees, so make sure your knowledge reflects this.

Finally, going freelance means abandoning any concept of job security. Clients will come and go as the wind, however, if you're able to keep a steady stream of them, you'll make a lot more than your in-house counterpart.

The Pros and Cons of Going Freelance

Let's look at what you'll be getting from becoming a freelancer first, shall we?

Pros

First of all, you get freedom, in more than one sense. The most important ones being location and time. You can work from anywhere you want. This is what caused the "digital nomad" lifestyle to crop up. That is where you abandon a constant physical location, and simply travel the world with your freelance income backing you.

This is a great way to live, and many people have whole-heartedly adopted it because of how comfortable it is to know that you can literally always just switch locations and go somewhere new. Having the freedom to go on an adventure whenever you want is extremely exciting.

On the other hand, this also has much more mundane applications. Has your day ever started badly because of your morning commute being cluttered or annoying? Well that's never going to happen again because your commute...doesn't exist! You just get out of bed...wait nevermind, you just lay IN your bed and work. This kind of freedom is generally unavailable to anyone but the richest in society, however, with freelancing, it's pretty easily possible.

Other than that, work often digs into your time when you don't want it to. This means that, for example, you wanted to go out with a friend at 9 a.m. but because of work, you were unable to. If you were a freelancer you wouldn't have this issue, as you'd be able to simply move all of your work to later in the day, and still go out with your friend. This also means that sometimes, if you had a really terrible day (eg. someone broke up with you), you can take a day off from work, as long as you make up for it later.

This is also great for productiveness, as everyone has different hours within the day that they consider themselves to be productive in. Rather than trying to fit into a company's working hours, you get to pick and choose your own.

The 2nd reason you should consider freelancing is money. Successful freelancers make a LOT more money than their desk-job counterparts. For example, some of the most successful freelance ethical hackers are raking in amounts that are in excess of $500,000 a year. Let that number sink in. On the flip side, it's not like the lead ethical hackers at companies aren't earning a lot, but it's usually not even half of that.

Obviously, this has some caveats. If you're getting employed by the FBI, you'll probably get offers that will put any freelancer to shame, but in order to get employed by the FBI you would have had to have a huge portfolio of freelance work beforehand.

For this reason, if all you're looking for is money, I'd suggest you consider freelancing much more strongly than working at a desk job position.

The 3rd reason to go freelance is, well, fun. Now, don't take me as one of those people that consider all work to be fun, but if you're a freelancer, you get to pick your opportunities.

Do you know that feeling when your boss assigns you a task you really hate, and you have to do it even though you'd rather do double that time, just working on something else? Well, as a freelancer, you don't have to do it. If there's a specific area of ethical hacking that you really dislike, then you can simply avoid it and never interact with it again in your life.

This freedom also lets you take bigger and better challenges. You don't have to wait for your boss to trust you with a task that they reckon is above your abilities. Just take it and give it a try! Worst case scenario, you don't live up to the client's expectations and your reputation takes a bit of a temporary hit.

Cons

The first con to freelancing is, well, the freedom. But wait, you say, didn't you say freedom was a pro? It is, if you can bear with it. It can be extremely easy to fall into the trap of not working enough, as you're not bound by contract, location, or anything similar.

This often leads to "freelancers," people that are actually unemployed, and have been holding onto their last job title and stapling freelancer next to it in hopes of making it sound better. After all, with nothing to chain you down, it can be very easy to fly too close to the sun.

The second pitfall (relatively similar to the first) many fall into is late assignments. Starting with the first time you say "Oh yeah this is going to be late" then everything henceforth cascades endlessly. From one assignment to the next. This can often even happen without agitating clients, but doing things at the last moment is generally a bad idea if for no other reason then for the stress that it causes. The stress itself often causes issues which cascade, meaning that if one day you were just a bit stressed out, the next you might be quite stressed, and afterwards you're having a meltdown.

Now, the third is finding clients. Finding clients is...hard, especially for those just starting out. In fact, if you're in a higher-class country (UK, US, Russia, etc.) then you might find that most entry-level jobs in your field of choice are paid under rate. While most freelancers do earn more than their desk job counterparts, this relationship flips on its head when it comes to entry level positions.

After all, an entry level job can usually be done just as well by someone from India (which has a low average wage) and someone from the US. Luckily, when it comes to ethical hacking, there are far more jobs than there are freelancers. This means that this kind of freelance rate depreciation doesn't really happen.

On the other hand, even if there are so many jobs, that doesn't mean it isn't difficult to reach clients, and that they aren't selective. Getting your very first freelance job is always really hard, which is why I'd recommend going for a desk job at first, at least until you've gotten your feet wet in the industry. This is because generally, when it comes to finding clients, people rely on experience. Freelancers will want to work with people connected to their past clients, and their past clients will be looking for freelancers with experience. As a general rule of thumb, experience is king in the freelancing world.

This brings us to another con of freelancing. Being your own boss is surprisingly hard. You need to be able to make your own website and make sure to advertise yourself. You need to pay attention to SEO as well as your skills in the actual field you're working in. While freelancing is a job that has very free hours, in a way, it's a 24/7 job in the sense that you never really get to stop working for a while.

How to Start Freelancing

Now, assuming you've gone past the pros and cons of freelancing and have decided to start, what do you need to do?(If you've decided it isn't for you, feel free to skip this part.)

Now, I'd like to split this up into two parts. In one of them I'll be recommending a road to someone that already has IT experience, while in the other I'll be gearing the text towards a complete novice.

I Have Experience, Now What?

Now, if you have experience, you've got a leg up on pretty much everyone that doesn't. The first thing you should do is make a website.

A website? Shouldn't a CV be enough? While yes, most office positions do only ask for a CV, keep in mind that you'll be competing against other people directly. This means that every point you've got on the competition looks great. You're also presenting less as an employee and more as a business partner, and what kind of business partner doesn't have a website?

The first question you should be asking yourself is "Do I have any close contacts?" Chances are, if you've been working in the IT industry, you know quite a few people with websites. In fact, with most IT professionals, this might even be the bulk of people you know. If this is the case, then great, you've got some potential clients right there. Reach out to all of these people one by one and check if they've been having issues with finding a cybersecurity professional.

If any say yes, then great! You've got your first gig, so make sure to completely nail it. If you do so, then they'll be sure to recommend you to their friends. This is the most important part of freelancing—making a network of useful contacts that can be clients whenever you come into a pinch. Make sure that all of your past employers/clients know what you're working as right now, and tell them to recommend you if anyone they know is having cybersecurity issues.

This is great because it:

Builds your reputation. You will become much more well-known in your field if even people that don't dabble in cybersecurity know your name. Furthermore, having people that are ready to vouch for your quality is an excellent sign for future clients.

It builds a consistent clientele. After you've gotten a few successful gigs, chances are, clients will start flowing in by themselves. Word of mouth spreads fast in tech circles, and quality cybersecurity professionals are very few.

So, what if your past clients don't give you any gigs? Or they simply aren't eager enough to recommend you to their acquaintances? In that case, go over to social media, and job sites like Indeed.

There are countless postings for remote/freelance cybersecurity experts and ethical hackers on these sites. Make sure that you're using these to their fullest potential. Put "ethical hacker," "penetration tester," or "cybersecurity expert" into your bio. Other than that, make sure you're using Linkedin, as it's very popular among recruitment managers, and sometimes even having a well-made profile is enough to get you a few potential clients.

Indeed is generally best for long-term remote positions, though it isn't too bad for freelance ones either. Keep in mind that Indeed is a numbers game. A lot of the listings are fake or outdated, so make sure you're applying to tons.

Now, if none of these have worked, then it's time to turn to an aggregate site. This would be a site like UpWork or Freelancer, which are sites designed to promote bidding among freelancers for jobs.

Generally, I'd advise against using these sites, as they tend to give out lower rates than individually found clients would. On the other hand, if you've got a good portfolio of experience, you'll soon move past the beginner-level jobs (of which there are many) and move onto jobs that are actually well paid.

I Have No Experience, What Do I Do?

If you've just gotten into the world of ethical hacking and have no experience whatsoever to speak of, do not despair. After all, you have a solid foundation of knowledge, and a drive to succeed!

In this case, I'd advise to have someone make your website for you. Chances are, you either don't know enough to do it yourself, or would lose yourself to options paralysis. If you feel like you know enough and are decisive enough to do it well, then by all means do it yourself. On the other hand, hiring a professional is always a good idea.

After you're done with that, I suggest having a few portfolio pieces. They can be practice work you did in university, or just stuff you did to mess around for fun, but the important part is for it to be something you can display to prospective clients.

At that point, go to one of the freelance aggregate sites like UpWork or Freelancer (out of these two, I'd recommend UpWork as it seems more professional) and start hunting for gigs. Don't be afraid if you're only getting accepted for low-paying gigs, as these sites are notoriously built on reputation and experience. Make sure that you're always moving up. Every one of your clients should be better-paying than your last one.

After you've amassed a considerable amount of experience on one of these sites, come back here and apply the advice in the "I have experience, now what?" section.

Bounties

In either case (with experience or not), bounties are a solid, if extremely difficult, way to earn money. Bounties are mainly geared towards those with experience, but there have been cases where they've been obtained by those with less experience.

A bounty is when a company decides it wants its cybersecurity to be tested, and then they let anyone have a go at it. If any white hat succeeds at cracking a company's defenses, then they get what is known as a "bounty." So, in essence, you'd be pretending to be a malicious cracker that is trying to get into the company's systems, and if you succeed, then you get money. Sounds good, doesn't it?

The thing with bounties, however, is that for less proficient hackers, they're often more hassle than it's worth. After all, those that are worth doing will usually be taken by the top 5% of hackers worldwide, rather than the average joe of the ethical hacking world.

Wait, hats? Yes, weirdly enough, out of all the things in the world, hackers are actually separated by hats. Now, as we've already explored, just because someone is a hacker, it doesn't mean they're involved in illegal activity or anything of the like. You'll find that most people, online or otherwise, refer to hackers under one of three labels. These are white, grey, and black hat. The grey hat is sometimes considered a specific subset of black. These are terms which were created in order to define different hackers based on what they do, and we touched on each briefly in the intro.

On a similar note, it can be quite hard to define "hacker," as the term's technical use is rather different from the way that it is used in most of pop culture. With that being said, we can definitely say that a hacker is someone that uses a hole in a digital system to find ways to exploit and receive personal gain from it. In the case of white hat hackers, this gain would either be money provided by the firm that hired them, or the satisfaction of knowing they did something good.

So, what exactly are the three hats of hackers and what do they do?

Black Hats

Black hat hackers, mostly referred to as "black hats," are those hackers that are most often featured in pop culture, TV shows, and movies. This is the type of hacker you think of when you hear the word hacker. Black hat hackers are those that will break the law, as well as break into a computer's security in order to pursue a selfish agenda. This can be something ranging from simply stealing credit card numbers to stealing whole identities off of people.

In other cases, this is simply done out of malice, so a black hat hacker might make a botnet purely for the sake of DDOS-ing the websites that they aren't particularly fond of.

Black hats not only fit the stereotype that hackers are criminals, but are also the reason for its existence. They are basically the PC equivalent of highly trained robbers. It's not hard to see why other hacker groups generally aren't very fond of black hats, as they besmirch the others' names.

Black hats are often those that find zero day vulnerabilities in a site's or company's security, and then sell it to other organizations, or simply use it for their own selfish agendas instead.

Zero Day Vulnerability?

A zero-day is a flaw in a given piece of either hardware, software, or firmware which isn't known to any of the parties which would otherwise be tasked with patching up said flaw. The term itself can refer either to the vulnerability in itself, or alternatively, an attack which gives 0 days between discovering the vulnerability and attacking. When a zero day vulnerability is made known to the public, then it will be known as an n-day or one-day vulnerability, both of which are equally dangerous.

Usually, when a flaw like this is detected, then the person that detected it will bring said flaw to the company whose software is flawed. Occasionally, they'll announce the flaw publicly in case they can't reach the company itself. This is usually done in the interest of patching up that hole.

Given some time, the company which made the program can usually fix it and distribute the patch for it. Sometimes, this will mean delaying the product a bit, but after all, is it not worth it to do that if it means it saves the company a lot of money? Even if the vulnerability is made public, it can often take black hats a while to actually become able to exploit it. In these scenarios, it's pretty much a race between the black hats and white hats.

On the other hand, sometimes it is a black hat that first discovers the vulnerability. If it isn't known in advance, then the white hats at the company won't have any idea that the exploit even exists before it is used against them. Usually, these companies will employ ethical hackers to try to find such zero-day vulnerabilities, so they can be fixed up before their product reaches the market.

Security researchers operate together with information vendors who will often agree to not share any zero-day vulnerability information until they're allowed. For example, Google's own Project Zero suggests that, if you should find a vulnerability as a person not employed by the company, you should wait at least 90 days before disclosing the vulnerability to the public. On the other hand, if the vulnerability is something really critical, then Google suggests that you should wait only about 7 days to see if the company will close up the gaping hole they accidentally left open. On the other hand, if the vulnerability is already being exploited, then fire away!

Black Hat Hacker Example

Much like in the opening scenes of a movie starring Daniel Craig, all the way back in 1994, Vladimir Levin used his laptop in his St. Petersburg apartment in order to commit the first internet bank heist in history.

He transferred $10 million from accounts of various Citibank clients to a variety of accounts he owned around the world. Fortunately, this heist didn't go all that well for Levin. He was captured and imprisoned only three years later. Of the $10 million that he stole, only $400,000 was never found. The way Levin did this was actually incredibly simple. He simply hacked into clients' calls, noted their account information, then just went and gave their money to himself.

White Hats

Hey, this is us! White hat hackers, also often referred to as ethical hackers, are the direct opposite of black hat hackers. They're also experts at compromising computer security systems, so much so that many of them used to be black hats in the past, and reformed. These are the hackers which could be black hats, but rather choose to use their skills and knowledge for good, and for ethical purposes rather than their own selfish motivations (although you could argue that the pursuit of good is selfish in and of itself).

Most white hats are employed by companies in order to try and "simulate" a black hat, so they will try to break into an organization's security systems as best they could. The organization then authorizes the white hat hackers to use their knowledge of security systems in order to compromise the whole organization. Does this sound like something a black hat would do? Precisely. They need to simulate exactly what a black hat hacker would do, so that they can know whether or not they'll be able to stop them before they've dealt significant damage to the company. The attacks of a white hat hacker are generally used in order to enhance the organization's defenses against cyberattacks. Usually, these two things will be done by the same people, however, some companies will have white hat hackers and cybersecurity professionals separate.

The method of impersonating a black hat hacker to gain access to a company's confidential files in order to help them with their system is known as penetration testing.

You'll find that white hat hackers that find vulnerabilities in securities would rather disclose the same to the developer of the program, rather than fulfilling their own selfish desires.

If you accidentally find a vulnerability as an ethical hacker, it is your moral obligation to report it to the developer. With this, you're allowing them to patch their product before a black hat hacker can get to it and ruin it entirely.

It's also worth noting that, like we mentioned before, some organizations pay bounties even for anonymous white hats that are good enough to get into their system. By doing this, they ensure that they're safe from any black hats that might've infiltrated their ranks as white hats, as well as reaching a wider audience.

White Hat Hacker Example

Kevin Mitnick is pretty much the face of the ethical hacking movement these days, however, that wasn't always the case. In fact, many speculate that the reason for his fame, as well as his skills, is due to the fact that his hat wasn't always precisely the whitest of them all.

26 years ago, in 1995, the police force caught Mitnick in a high-profile arrest. He had been committing a spree of hacking activities that lasted for over 2 years. All of it was entirely illegal. Some of his exploits were truly massive. For example, during one of his escapades, he broke into the security systems of the Digital Equipment Corp. Once he was in, he decided to copy everything that was there, and copy he did.

After serving his jail sentence, he got some supervised release time, but before his time was even done, Mitnick had gone back to his old ways. In fact, before his punishment was served, he got entry into the Pacific Bell voicemail computers. It is thought that he got into several other places illegally, using methods like intercepting passwords, though this was never actually confirmed.

He got a solid 46 months for that, and 22 on top of that because he violated the time where he was supposed to be in supervised release. This was what finally marked the end of his career as a black hat hacker.

After serving his sentence, back in 2000, Mitnick decided he'd become a white hat hacker. He elected to become a paid consultant, and consult he did. Fortune 500 companies and even the FBI flocked to Mitnick for help. After all, he had a trove of talents and knowledge to share. There have been tons of people flocking to him over the years in order to learn from the experience he had. The knowledge and ideas that he possessed were then transitioned into his highly popular public speaking and writing work.

Mitnick has even taught classes himself, leading social engineering classes to possess the same knowledge that he used to. These were vital skills that we still need today. Even today, Mitnick is busy doing penetration tests, though now it's for some of the world's most successful and powerful companies.

Gray Hats

Nothing in life is black or white. Moving on, that unfunny joke is actually quite reflective of hacking. In fact, much like in life, there's always a grey area between white and black in the world of hacking.

As you should have guessed, a grey hat hacker sits in the awkward spot between a black hat hacker and a white hat. The grey hat hacker isn't exactly working for their own personal gain, or even just to do damage, but they do sometimes commit crimes, and do things that others might deem unethical. At other times, they're those that do something that's illegal, but at the same time, ethical.

Let's try to explain this. A black hat hacker is the kind of person that will get into a computer system without getting permission from anyone, and then proceed to steal the data that is inside it in order to achieve some kind of personal gain, or in order to vandalize the system. A white hat would ask for permission, they would test the system's security only after receiving it, and they wouldn't do anything with that other than inform the organization about the vulnerability, as well as how to fix it.

On the other hand, a grey hat hacker wouldn't do any of these things most of the time. While they didn't do it for malicious purposes, they still broke into a system without permission. At one end of the spectrum, a grey hat hacker would simply do this for fun, at which point they're much closer to black hat than white hat. On the other hand, they might have also done it to help the organization, even without permission, in which case they'd be much closer to white hat.

In case a grey hat hacker discovers a gaping security hole, it's hard to guess what they'd do. Anything between simply doing nothing, to alerting the company directly, would be possible. On the other hand, the "average" response, I'd reckon, is revealing the flaw publicly so that the company will have the time to fix it, but also not bothering enough to contact them directly.

It's worth noting that all of these things fall into the water if this is done for personal gain. In that case, this falls into black hat behavior. Even if the public disclosure later causes chaos (because a black hat found it) or helps the company (because a white hat found it), that doesn't change anything for the grey hat.

Grey Hat Hacker Example

In August of 2013, Khalil Shreateh was an unemployed computer security expert. He decided he'd hack the Facebook page of Mark Zuckerberg. The, Mark Zuckerberg. Surprisingly, he was successful. Facebook's CEO was forced to face something that Khalil had been telling them about for quite a while.

The truth was that Khalil had discovered a bug that allowed people to post to pretty much anyone's page without their consent. He tried, with no avail, to inform Facebook of this. After getting told repeatedly that this was not a bug, Khalil took the matter into his own hands.

Khalil hacked into the CEO's page and pointed out how much of an issue this bug could be. After all, malicious spammers could use it for a variety of things, and that's only scratching the surface of potential abuses that this could have.

After this happened, Facebook finally decided to correct this issue, which could have caused them millions in losses. Unfortunately, Khalil didn't get any compensation for his work from Facebook's White Hat program, which was due to him needing to violate their policies to find the issue.

As well as knowing what the terms mean, it is important to note that people can be multiple hats, and that the terms can be used for behavior, rather than just people. For example, someone could both do penetration testing for one company, while also hacking into another maliciously. This would make them both a black and a white hat hacker.

Behavior is much easier to understand when it's explained. Basically, ask yourself the question, "If a person did this every day, which kind of hacker would they be considered?" And you've got your answer as to what kind of hacker they are.

CHAPTER 5: ETHICAL HACKING EXPLAINED

When it comes to security, being a hacker is one of the most overused terms. It appears everywhere, and even the entertainment industry and many authors use it often in their films, books, TV shows, and other media forms. Because of this, the word "hacker" is mostly viewed as a bad profession and always connected to shady or real criminal activities. So, when people hear that someone is involved in hacking, they immediately see that person as somebody who doesn't have good intentions. They are mostly represented as "operators from the shadow", even antisocial. On the other hand, they are also viewed as a social activist. This label became especially popular after a few affairs such as WikiLeaks. Many hackers were involved in obtaining many important documents from governments, politicians, and corporations that showed information that was very different from that given to the public. Also, organized groups such as Anonymous or Lizard Squad had a huge influence on the perception of hackers in recent years.

The Evolution of Hacking

Initially, hacking appeared out of curiosity. Technology enthusiasts wanted to know how systems worked and what they could do with them. Today, we also have many of those who like to experiment, customize, and improve original designs. In the early 1970s, hackers were actually people who could have been found in their houses taking apart radios, early computers, and other devices of that era and figuring out how they worked. With the progress of technology, this kind of individuals advanced along with it. Later, in the 1980s when the PC was the highest achievement of technology, hackers moved to that environment and even started to engage in more suspicious activities, often malicious. The reason for this was also the fact that the attacks could impact more systems since more and more people had PCs. When the Internet became a thing in the 1990s, all of the systems connected to it became interconnected, too. The result was obvious - curiosity mixed with bad intentions was now available worldwide and since it was easier to hack different computer systems, more and more hackers appeared.

At the beginning of the 21st century, computers stopped being the only devices that could be hacked. In the meantime, we acquired other technologies such as smartphones, Bluetooth devices, tablets, and many other things that hackers could use as their targets. It is very simple. Not only does technology evolve, hackers do, too. So, if the system is complicated, the hacker's attack is going to be harder to escape. And when the Internet started to be a part of everything that we do, different types of data became easier to access. The first hackers' internet attacks in the 1990s were usually connected to website defacements and many of these cyberspace attacks ended up being pranks, sometimes funny and interesting, but sometimes they ended up being very serious, even criminal activities. More aggressive attacks started to occur such as hacking websites of different governments, or something that you are probably more familiar with – hacking of film websites that resulted in many pirate websites that are active even today.

As we already mentioned, from the beginning of the 2000s cyberspace attacks became more frequent and more malicious. Additionally, these attacks were progressing fast. At the time, there were already hacking activities classified as advances. Many of these hackers had criminal motives and even though we can't say that there is a standard classification for them, we will set them in several categories:

- There were hackers who used their skills to manipulate stock prices which caused many financial complications

- Some of them hacked people's personal data, thus they were stealing identities

- One of the most frequent hacker attacks was connected to credit card theft or cyberspace vandalism

- Also, as we mentioned before, piracy was quite common and at some point even popular

- The last but not the least type of hacking attack that was usually from the early 2000s was a denial of service and service attacks.

As you know, over the last few decades, most financial transactions have been made online, which is a tempting field for crooks. But not only that, the openness of mobile phones, laptops, tablets, and similar devices that we use daily also increased the space and how every kind of information can be stolen. An increasing number of internet users, users of different gadgets, and similar software products that connect people and their devices in multiple ways increased the number of those who have an interest in obtaining some part of it.

All of these mischievous activities over the years resulted in new laws in almost every country in the world. These laws emerged from the need to gain control over cyberspace criminal activities. Although the number of website hackings became lower, organized cybercrime increased.

Examples: Mischief or Criminal?

Hacking is by no means a phenomenon that appeared overnight. It existed in different forms and evolved all the way from the 1960s. However, in the beginning, it was never addressed as a criminal activity. We will view a few cases that will give you a closer look at some of the attacks, and generic examples that gradually changed that picture.

One of the most famous hacking groups in the world called the "Anonymous" appeared in 2003. They were responsible for a series of attacks on government websites and other networks. They also hacked many news agencies and other organizations. These multiple successful intrusions ranked them among one of the most active cyber organized groups ever. The interesting thing is that they are still active and committed to attacking high-profiled targets.

During the mid-2000s, a new computer virus was discovered. The name of this virus was Stuxnet and it had a specific design that attacked only systems that had any kind of connection with the production of uranium. The unique feature of this program was the fact that it ignored other systems, and it attacked only if the requirements mentioned above were met.

Another interesting case is the case of a young Russian hacker named Kristina Vladimirovna Scechinskaya who was involved in a plot to defraud some of the biggest banks in Great Britain and the United States. The whole thing started in 2009 when she used the famous "Trojan horse" virus to open thousands of accounts while attacking others. The total amount of the money that she succeeded in stealing in the scam was 3 billion dollars. She was called the world's sexiest hacker, which helped with breaking the stereotype of hackers being antisocial beings living in the basement and so forth.

All of these cases are some of the most famous high-profile hacking incidents that happened, even though maybe some of them didn't gain that much media coverage. In fact, many of the cybercriminal cases that appear in the news stay unresolved, but many others had a huge impact on different industries but never make it to the breaking news or ended up persecuted for cybercrime.

Now that we have reviewed some concrete incidents, we will name some of the other activities that are considered to be cybercrimes. We will call them generic examples, but keep in mind that these are not the only ones. Many other forms can be viewed as illegal.

- Gaining access to any services or resources that you don't have permission for. This is mostly referred to as stealing usernames and passwords. There are some cases in which obtaining this information without permission is considered a cybercrime even if you don't use them or they are the accounts of friends or family members.

- There is a form of digital trespassing called Network intrusions that is also considered to be a cybercrime. In essence, just like ordinary trespassing, this means that you went someplace without permission to enter (or in this case access). So in the case where someone acquires access to a system or group of systems without authorization we can say that the person violated the network, thus committed cybercrime. Still, some network intrusions can happen without using hacker tools. Sometimes logging into guest accounts without previous authorization can be viewed as cybercrime.

- One of the most complex, yet one of the simplest forms of hacking is by going after the most vulnerable element in the system – humans. This form of cybercrime is known as social engineering, and we say that it can be simply because the person may be a far more accessible component of the system than any other, and it is easier to interact with. However, people can give cues that are difficult to understand whether they are spoken or not, which makes it hard for the hacker to get the information that they need.

- The issue of posting or transmitting illegal materials became difficult to deal with in general, especially in the last decade. Social media gained much attention and many other services that are internet-related increased in usage and popularity. This enabled many illegal materials to go from one place to another in the shortest time possible, thus it can spread very fast

- Fraud is also a thing that often happens, especially on the Internet, and it is also considered to be a cybercrime. Just like the original term, fraud in cyberspace also means that a party or parties were deceived typically for the purpose of financial gain or causing damage.

What Does it Mean to be an Ethical Hacker?

All of the things that we previously mentioned in this chapter referred to hackers in general. However, the real goal is to learn how to be an ethical hacker and explore the skills that one should have.

Ethical hackers are people employed usually by organizations to test their security. They usually work through direct employment or through temporary contracts. The key is that they use the same skills as all other hackers, but there is one big difference- they have permission to attack the system directly from the system's owner. Additionally, being an ethical hacker means that you reveal the weaknesses of the system you evaluated (because every system in the world has them) only to the owner and to no one else. Furthermore, organizations or individuals that hire ethical hackers use very strict contracts that specify which parts of the system are authorized for an attack and which are off-limits. The role of an ethical hacker also depends on the job that he or she is entitled to, thus the needs of the employer. Nowadays, some organizations have teams that are permanent staff members and their job is to perform ethical hacking activities.

Hackers can be divided into 5 categories. Keep in mind that this categorization may vary, but we can say that these are the most common ones:

- The first category is also known as "Script Kiddies". These hackers usually don't have any training or they do, but very limited. They know how to use only some of the basic hacking tools and techniques and since they are not skillful enough, it can happen that sometimes even they don't fully understand their doings or the consequences that their work might have.

- The second category involves hackers known as "White Hat hackers". They attack the computer system, but they are the good guys which means that they cause no harm to their work. These kinds of hackers are most frequently ethical hackers, but they can be pen-testers too.

- "Grey Hat hackers" are the third hacker category. As their name suggests, they are in between being good and bad but their final decision is to choose the good side. Still, these kinds of hackers have difficulties gaining trust since they can act suspicious.

- The fourth category that we will mention in this section is labeled as the "Black Hat hackers". This category refers to the hackers that we mentioned before in this chapter. These people usually work on the "other side" of the law and they are usually connected to criminal activities.

- Last but not least are the "Suicide hackers". They are called this because their goal is to prove the point, and that is why they want to knock out their target. These hackers don't worry about being caught because their purpose is not to hide but to prove, so they are easier to find.

Responsibilities of an Ethical Hacker

The most important thing that an ethical hacker should learn and never forget is that he or she always needs to have permission for any kind of system attack. The ethical code that you need to implement in every task as an ethical hacker says that no network or system should be tested or targeted if you don't own it or if you don't own permission for it. Otherwise, you can be seen as guilty for multiple crimes that can happen in the meantime. Firstly, that can harm your career, and secondly, if it's something very serious, it can even threaten your freedom, too.

The smartest thing to do is to have a contract from your employer close at the time of testing or attacking the required target. The contract represents a written authorization, but you have to keep in mind that you are allowed to examine only the parts of the system specified in that contract. So, if your employer wants to give you permission to hack additional parts of the system or to remove authorization for some, he should alter the contract first, and you shouldn't operate further until you get the new permit. Note that the only thing that distinguishes an ethical hacker from the cybercriminal is the contract. Therefore, you should always pay special attention to the verbiage that deals with privacy and confidentiality issues because it often happens that you come across intimate information of your client whether business or personal.

That is one more reason why your contract should include to whom you can talk about the things you found while examining the system and who is forbidden to hear any updates from you. In general, clients usually want to be the only people who know everything you eventually find out.

An organization known as EC Council (International Council of Electronic Commerce Consultants) is one of the most important organizations when it comes to regulation of these issues. According to them, an ethical hacker has to keep private any kind of information acquired during work and treat it as confidential. This is especially pointed out for client's personal information, which means that you are not allowed to transfer, give, sell, collect, or do something similar with any of the client's information such as Social Security number, email address, home address, unique identifier, name, and so forth. The only way you can give this kind of information to a third party is to have written consent from your employer (client).

Even though some might argue about the distinctions of hackers and ethical hackers, the division is quite straightforward- hackers are separated by their intentions. This means that those who intend to do harm and use their skills to access data without permission are labeled as black hats, while those who work with their client's consent are considered to be white hat hackers. Naming these two categories "the bad one" and "the good one" can be controversial, so we will try to adhere to these expressions in the following manner:

- Black hats typically work outside the law which means that they don't have authorization from the person referred to as "the client" to consent to their activities.

- Contrarily, white hats do have authorization and consent from the person referred to as "client" and they even keep the information they have between the client and white hats alone.

- Gray hats, on the other hand, cross into both of these territories and they use both kinds of actions at different periods.

Hacktivists are a category of hackers that we haven't mentioned before. They belong to the movement known as Hacktivism which refers to actions that hackers use to impact the general public by promoting a certain political agenda. So far, hacktivists have been involved with agencies, big corporations, and governments.

Ethics and Code of Conduct for Hackers

Like every other profession, even hacking has its Code of Conduct that sets rules which can help clients (individuals or organizations) to evaluate if the person that deals with their networks and computer systems, in general, is trustworthy. The organization that has conducted this Code was already mentioned in the previous sections and it is known as EC-Council. Obtaining a CEH credential from the EC-Council means that you fully understand the expectations that you need to abide by. We have provided some parts of the code, so make sure you read it and familiarize yourself with it.

- Information that you gain during your professional work should be kept confidential and private (especially personal information)

- Unless you have your client's consent, you can't give, transfer, or sell the client's home address, name, or other uniquely identifying information.

- You have to protect the intellectual property, yours and that of others, by using skills that you acquired on your own so that all of the benefits go to its original creator.

- Be sure to disclose to the authorized personnel any danger that you suspect can come from the Internet community, electronic transactions, or other hardware and software indicator.

- Make sure that the services you provide are in the area of your expertise, thus you work honestly while being aware of any potential limitations that might be a consequence of your education or experience.

- You should work only on projects that you are qualified for and do jobs that match your skills in terms of training, education, and work experience.

- You mustn't knowingly use any software obtained illegally or retained unethically.

- You can't participate in any financial practices that can be viewed as deceptive such as double billing, bribery, and so on.

- Make sure that you use the client's property properly, without crossing the limits set on your contract.

- You should disclose a potential conflict of interest to all parties concerned, especially if that conflict can't be avoided.

- Make sure that you provide good management for the entire project that you are working on including activities for promotion and risk disclosure.

CHAPTER 6: HOW TO SCAN YOUR SYSTEM

There are several ways to scan your computer. However, it is important to understand that different scans pursue a different type of data, thus achieve different results. That is why you should look into the scan more carefully before you go into that kind of process. Scans, in general, share a similar theme which is based on the premise that its purpose is to collect information about one or more hosts. Still, if you dig deeper, you will see that some differences emerge along the way. Every scan gives different feedback on the type of data it gains, therefore, each one is valuable in its own way. To avoid complicating things we will use simple categorization and say that there are three categories and that they all have their specific characteristics.

Port Scan

The first category that we will mention is called the port scan. This is a process in which packets or messages are carefully sent to the computer that you are targeting. The intention of this scan is data gathering and these probes are most frequently connected to the number of ports or those types that have less or equal to 1024 ones. If this technique is applied carefully, there are many things that you can learn about the possibilities that a system that you are scanning has to offer to the whole network. You can even find differences between systems such as controllers of domains, web servers, mail servers, and so on, during the process. One of the most commonly used port scanners is known as Fyodor's map. Port scanning is one of the most used types of scanning and it often happens that other people assume that you talk about port scanning just by mentioning the "scan" term.

Network Scan

Network scan is the second category of scanning that we'll mention. It is designed specifically to find all hosts that are "live" on a certain network which means that this scan will find all of the hosts that are running through the system at the time. It will identify which systems might be targeted or find hosts that can scan further. These kinds of scans are known as ping sweeps too, and they can scan the IPs' range very fast and then establish if the address had a host that is powered-on attached to it. The most common example of a network scan is Angry IP, but there are many others used to achieve the same goal.

Vulnerability Scan

The third category is known as vulnerability scan and it is used to find all of the weaknesses of the targeted system. The most common reason to use this kind of scan is if the client wants proactive measures, especially if there is a doubt that someone might attack it. The goal of those who want a vulnerability scan is to intentionally grasp the situation about potential problems and act on them as fast as possible. Classic vulnerability scans gain information about access points, hosts, ports (especially the opened ones); it analyzes the response of all services, generates reports, and as a very important feature it classifies threats if there are any. They are popular among large corporations because they can be used to find easy access to the system. The two most frequently used vulnerability scanners are Rapid7 Nexpose and Tenable Nessus. Additionally, there are many specialized scanners on the market, and the most famous ones are Nikto, Burp Suite, WebInspect, and so forth.

To avoid potential misunderstandings that can appear before an ethical hacker, you should know the difference between penetration testing and vulnerability. First of all, vulnerability scan has the purpose of finding out the weaknesses that a host or a network has, but it doesn't exploit the weak points it finds. On the other hand, penetration tests go a step further and not only can find the same weaknesses but uses them, intending to find out how far an attacker could go if they find them, too.

You probably wonder what kind of information a penetration test provides. The answer can't be simple; still, some general assumptions can be made. When you scan a system, it is highly probable that you will encounter many different data sets. We can list them as follows to make it easier:

- **Network's live hosts**
- **Architecture of the system**

- Opened and closed ports and information that the host has on the operating system (or more systems)
- **Running processes on the host system**
- Type of system's weaknesses and their level
- **Patches that the target system has**
- **Information on firewalls' presence**
- Routers and their addresses along with other information

When you take a closer look, it is clear why many people define scanning as a type of intelligence-gathering process that can be used by real attackers. If you are creative and skillful enough you can perform a successful scan. However, if you hit a roadblock while scanning, your skills have to come in and you have to see what your next move will be. Keep in mind that once you gather information, it will take some time to analyze it, and that also depends on how good you are at reading the results that the scan gave you. The more knowledge you have, the easier it will be to decipher results.

Live Systems Check

Let's begin with finding the targets that you'd probe and investigate. Keep in mind that even though you gained information about the range of IP or IPs that are owned by your client (individual or organization), it doesn't mean that each of those IP addresses will have a host that is connected to it. The first thing you need to do if you want to have meaningful progress is to find which "pulses" are real and which aren't, thus which IPs have hosts. The question is, how will you check if there are live systems in the environment that you target? The answer is actually simple. There are many ways to do that. Still, the ones that are most commonly used are port scanning, war dialing, pinging and wardriving. Each of these techniques has its own value since they all provide certain information that is unique to their designs. Once you learn more about them, you will understand how they work and what differences they have and it will be easier to implement the one you need more for a penetration test.

War Dialing

War dialing is an old but useful way to scan the system. It was practically unchanged from the 1980s and the reason why it's still used is because it has proven to be one of the most reliable and useful tools for information gathering. When it comes to practice, this technique is quite straightforward in comparison to other scanning forms. War dialing works on the principle of dialing a block of different phone numbers while using modems that are considered to be standard. Once the scan dials the numbers, it can determine the locations of the systems that also have their modem attached and that are accepting connections. At first glance it may seem that this is an old-fashioned mechanism, however, it is more than useful on multiple levels. The main one is the fact that modems are still widely used since they are affordable and have good phone lines that are basically everywhere.

One of the reasons why modems are still in usage is that they serve as a backup to the existing technologies. So if other connectivity options fail, lines provided by phones will be available to prevent major outages. For corporations, it is a good deal because it is affordable and it gives some type of security in case something really big happens.

So, the question that follows is what happens when you find a modem. Firstly, you need to be familiarized with the devices that are commonly connected to modems nowadays. For example, PBXs (Private Branch Exchanges) frequently have non-digital modes attached to them. These kinds of modems are good for different kinds of mischief from an attacker. However, some modems have firewalls attached to them, or fax machines, routers, and so on. So when attackers gain access through a firewall, the environment of the device won't be protected for long. You should be mindful of pivot points when accessing the system. Pivot points are systems that are compromised and then used to attack other systems, making their environment unsafe. Over the years, many programs have been created as war dialing programs. The best-known ones are:

Tone Loc, which is a program based on looking for dial tones by dialing random numbers that are within an attacker's range. This program can also search for the carrier frequency of a modem. It takes inputs with area codes and number ranges that an attacker wants to dial.

PhoneSweep from Niksun, which is a program that represents one of the few options that are commercially available on the market.

THC-SCAN ADOS, which is a program based on dialing phone numbers using modems and looks for a carrier frequency from that modem.

Ping

Another commonly used tool for scanning is called ping. Ping is used to determine the connectivity of a network by establishing if the remote host is located up or down. Although it is a quite simple feature, it is still highly efficient for the initial process of scanning. Ping is based on ICMP (Internet Control Message Protocol) messages and that is why this kind of scanning is sometimes called an ICMP scan. It works simply. One system sends an echo (in this case an ICMP echo) to another system and if it's alive, it will reply by sending another ICMP echo as a response. When the initial system receives this reply, it confirms that the target is live or up.

Ping tells you not only if the target is alive, but it also gains information on the speed of target packets and TTL (time to live) data. If you want to use ping in Windows, you should just enter the following prompt command: ping or ping. The Linux versions use the same command, but the command will constantly ping the target unless you press ctrl+c to stop the process.

Even though you can use ping to access hostnames and IP addresses, it is recommended that you ping by IP address rather than hostname technique first because inactive hostname might mean that there is a DNS issue rather than an unavailable system. Keep in mind that if you have a system to ping, you ping it, and don't receive a response although you know that the targeted system is working, the targeted system may have a disabled ping service. If that is true, you won't receive any response from that type of system at all.

Ports and Checking Their Status

When you locate the network's live systems, the next step is to take a look at the hosts once again. The goal is to determine whether they have any open ports or not. Generally speaking, what you are doing is zooming in on every live host that you've previously found and examining the ports to establish if any of them are opened. However, in this phase, you can only see if there are opened or closed ports, but you can't do anything about it since that advanced feature comes in some more advanced sections. Remember that knowing the ports and port scans is one of the essential skills for ethical hacking and when you examine different types of port scans that exist, you will know in which situations you'll prefer one over another. Be mindful of details because, at the end of the day, studying is the best way to improve your skills.

CHAPTER 7: PENETRATION TESTING

Penetration testing, also known as pen testing, is one of the main activities ethical hackers do. A penetration test is also called a white hat attack due to the fact that it is done by a white hat hacker for the purpose of helping out a system's owner. It is a process of finding vulnerabilities in applications, networks, and systems that could potentially be exploited by malicious users that are trying to get into the system. The process can be executed manually, but it can also be automated through the use of other applications. No matter how you do it, the goal of the process always stays the same. First, you gather as much information as possible about the target before starting the test. This boils down to finding entry points and attempting to break into the system, as well as collecting the findings into one document.

No matter how you approach the process, its goal always remains the same: to find weaknesses in the security of a system. This is mostly done digitally, but can also be done in the physical part of computer security. As you know, there are methods of hacking that involve using the staff in order to get into the system. Penetration testing can be used to test how much employees are aware of security policies, as well as how quickly an organization can recognize a threat.

After the ethical hacker has identified the exploitable weaknesses of a system, they notify the IT and network system managers of the organization. Based on this, these experts can take measures that will help out with the security of their systems, as well as allocate the necessary resources for this.

The Purpose of Penetration Testing

The main goal of a penetration test is finding out if the system has any vulnerabilities that could be abused to destabilize the system's security, as well as see if the security complies with the standard and test how well the employees of a company know the security issues. This is done in order to determine how the organization would be affected by a potential break in, as well as how the vulnerabilities can be fixed.

This can also lead to discovering the faults in the security policies of a company. Some companies, for example, have many policies regarding the detection and prevention of a hacking attack, but have none regarding how to expel the hacker.

Cloud Pen Testing Responsibilities

In some networks you might find different combinations of on-premises systems and cloud systems. This means that the pen testing responsibilities tend to vary between different networks.

We have already mentioned how important reports are in penetration testing. They will usually give the company a lot of helpful insight into their security system and help them prioritize the improvements to the security system they had planned. These reports give app developers the incentive to create more secure applications. By understanding how hackers get into their applications, the developers can educate them further on how to make their future projects more secure so that similar vulnerabilities do not pop up ever again.

How Often Should You Perform Penetration Tests?

Usually, companies do this on a regular basis. This is typically done once a year. The more often they do penetration testing, the more efficient the work of the security and IT management gets. On top of the regularly executed penetration tests, companies also do them when:

- The company adds a new infrastructure or application to their system
- The company makes large modifications to their system
- The company adds new offices in a different location
- **The company adds new security patches**
- **The company modifies its security policies**

You should realize, however, that penetration testing doesn't go the same for every company. How pen testing goes depends on many factors like:

- How large is the company? The larger the presence of a company, the higher the chance of the company being under attack by a hacker, as they have more attack approaches and juicier pay-offs.

- How much money can the company give for penetration testing? Smaller companies cannot always afford to do them on a yearly basis due to the fact that the process can cost quite a bit of money. Only the more lucrative companies to it on a yearly basis, while the smaller ones do it once every two years.

- What does the law say? In some industries, there are laws that require companies to do security tasks.

- Some companies have their infrastructures in the cloud. Sometimes these companies cannot run their own penetration tests and the responsibility falls onto the provider himself.

Every company has different needs when it comes to penetration testing. This is why white hat hackers need to be very flexible when it comes to penetration testing, as their efforts will be more efficient if the penetration testing they do is tailored to the company they are working for. After every penetration test, it is recommended to run several more follow-up tests to make sure that the results are noted in the penetration tests that are yet to come.

Penetration Testing Tools

Penetration testing can be automated due to the number of tools that are available today. These tools are usually used by pen testers in order to quickly scan the system for common vulnerabilities. They are used to scan code to find malicious parts which can be used to breach the system. They find vulnerabilities in the system by examining the encryption techniques and hard-coded values.

Penetration Test Strategies

Whenever a white hat hacker is approaching a penetration test, they should always define the scope in which they will operate. This usually tells the tester which parts of the system they should approach, as well as which tools and techniques should be used while working. This helps allocate resources and manpower more efficiently while doing a penetration test.

If a penetration tester that was hired by the company gains access to the system because they found a password of an employee in plain sight, this tells the security team that the security practices of the employee are lacking and show where improvements need to be made.

There are many strategies that penetration testers use relatively often:

- ### Targeted testing

The company's IT team is usually in charge of targeted testing. They work in tandem with the penetration testers in order to do this. This approach is sometimes referred to as the "lights turned on" approach due to the fact that everyone has access to the results and execution of this test.

- ### External testing

External testing is executed in order to find weaknesses in the parts of the system that are visible from the exterior. This includes firewalls, web servers, email servers, and domain names. The objective of this kind of penetration test is to find out if that part of the system can be used to access the deeper parts of the system and how far the hacker can get during that attack.

- ### Internal testing

An attack performed during internal testing starts from behind the firewall and is done by a user that has standard access privileges. This is usually done in order to see what extent of damage can be done by an employee of the company that has malicious intents.

- ## Blind Testing

Blind testing has this name because the information available to the tester is greatly limited due to the fact that it is made to emulate what kind of path a real attacker would take in a quick job. These testers are used to emulate an actual all-out attack that a malicious individual from outside the company would commit and are given almost nothing other than the name of the company that is hiring them. This kind of test can take quite a bit of time due to the time the hacker needs to find where they can access the system, which makes it cost quite a pretty penny.

- ## Double-blind

This is a step-up on the blind test. The double-blind test is a kind of test where only a few people within the organization know that the test is being executed. The employees are not told where or when the attack will happen or who will execute it. This kind of test is very useful due to the fact that it gives some very useful insight into the organization's security monitoring, as well as the efficiency at which the employees execute the instructed procedures.

- ## Black box testing

This penetration test requires the tester to have no information on the target. It is another variation of the blind test. The tester is instructed to act like an actual attacker and has to find their own entry point and deduce which techniques and tools should be used for the job.

- ## White box testing

White box testing gives the testers great insight into the important information about the system of the company that they are hired to attack. This information can go anywhere from the IP addresses, to the source code, to the infrastructure schematics. The information provided can be flexible depending on the needs of the company.

It is important for every penetration testing team to use different kinds of tests in order to find all of the weaknesses they can. This, in turn, tells them which kinds of attacks could deal the most damage to the system.

Using different pen testing strategies helps pen testing teams focus on the desired systems and gain insight into the types of attacks that are most threatening.

Penetration Testing Cloud-based Applications

As I have mentioned before, due to the growth of cloud storage, many companies have been moving their infrastructures from on-premise to cloud storage. Due to how cloud itself works, white hat hackers had to develop new techniques and discover some new and interesting angles when approaching penetration testing. The problem with applications that run in the cloud is the fact that there are several obstacles when it comes to pen testing. Both legal and technical problems might occur when you are aiming to check the security of the application. Here is how you, as a beginner, should approach white hat hacking on cloud.

Step 1: Make sure to understand how the cloud provider's policies work

As we know, there are private and public clouds. We will focus on the public side today, as they have their own policies when it comes to penetration testing. A white hat hacker will always have to wait for the confirmation of the provider before executing the test. This puts many limitations on what can be done as a part of the process. To be more precise, whenever you want to pen test an application that is running on a public cloud, you need to do a great deal of research as to which techniques are recommended and allowed by the provider. If you do not follow the procedures that the provider has set, you can get in a load of trouble. For example, your test can sometimes seem like an actual attack which can result in your account being permanently shut down.

Any anomaly in a cloud will be spotted by the provider, who looks for anomalies constantly. Sometimes you might receive a call from someone to check what is going on. More often, however, you will be met with a line of automated procedures that will shut the system down if your actions are perceived as an attack. This can lead to several bad things, like all of your cloud-stored systems and data going offline and you having a lot to explain to your provider before they bring them back online.

Another thing that can happen if you conduct your penetration tests irresponsibly is that you run the risk of affecting other users. There is always the possibility that you will put a load on the resources used by other users while you are pen testing. This is a problem with public clouds, as there are always multiple active users, so not all of the system can be dedicated to one user. This can lead to outrage from the provider, too. They might call you in a not-so-friendly manner or just shut down your account.

To make a long story short, there are rules when you want to poke around public clouds. You will have to keep the legal requirements in mind, along with all of the procedures and policies that the provider instructs you to. If you do not do this, you will face some headaches.

Step 2: Come in with a plan

Whenever you want to run a penetration test on a cloud, you need to come in with a plan. In your plan you are going to have to cover:

- Application(s): Get acquainted with APIs and user interfaces
- Data access: Understand how the data will react to the test
- Network access: Understand how the data and the application are protected by the system
- Virtualization: Make sure to measure how your workload will be handled by virtual machines
- Compliance: Get acquainted with the regulations and laws that you will have to respect while running the penetration test.
- Automation: Select which tools you will be using while executing the penetration tests
- Approach: See which admins you will involve in the pen testing. There are benefits to not notifying the admins. This gives insight into how the

admins would react during an actual attack. This approach is highly resented by most admins.

If you are working as part of a team, you should plan the approach together with the rest of the team and make sure that everyone will follow every part of the plan. The entire team should make sure to not stray away from it, as it could result in all of your efforts being for nothing due to the admin killing your access to the system.

Step 3: Pick out which tools you will use

The market provides you with many tools that can be used in penetration testing. In the past, pen testing on clouds was done via on-premise tools. Recently, however, many tools were made that are specially used for cloud pen testing and will prove to be a cheaper option. Another benefit of these tools is the fact that they leave a small hardware footprint.

What you need to know about these tools is the fact that they simulate actual attacks. There are many automated processes which can pick out vulnerabilities in a system. Hackers have done automated activities like guessing passwords and looking for APIs in order to get into a system. Your job is to simulate these activities.

Sometimes, these tools cannot do everything you might need them to do. Your last resort is usually to write a penetration system of your own. This should always be avoided as much as possible as it could set you back quite a bit.

Step 4: Observe the response

While you are running a penetration test, you will have to keep a close eye on:

- Human response - When it comes to cloud penetration testing, you will always have to track how the admins and users will react to your test. Many will immediately shut the system down in order to avoid damage done to it. Other admins will first try to diagnose the situation in order to identify the threat and the solution to anything similar. You should also keep a close eye on how people react in your client provider.

- Automated response - The first thing you should look at is how the system itself will react to your penetration test. Thee system will spot you and react to you. These reactions can range anywhere from a block of an IP address to your whole system being shut down. No matter how this goes down you need to alert admins that are in charge of applications and security in order to see what actions they took and what happened in their areas.

Both of these responses need to be documented. Once you document your findings and take them into consideration, you will finally see where the weaknesses in the system are and how secure the system is.

Step 5: Find and eliminate vulnerabilities

The final product of penetration testing is a list of vulnerabilities that the team has spotted. There can be a vast amount of issues, while sometimes there can be few or none. If you find none, you might have to run another test in order to re-evaluate the results of the previous one.

The vulnerabilities you might find in penetration tests of cloud applications will usually look similar to the following:

Access application data allowed using xxxxx API.

- **API access granted after 20 attempts.**

- Password generator detected during access of an application.

- **Encryptions do not comply with regulations.**

The issues will almost always be different depending on which application you are testing and what kind of test you executed.

Do not forget that there are different layers to the test. All of the parts like network, storage system, database, etc. are all tested separately. The issues, in turn, are also reported separately. You should always run a test with all of the layers together in order to see how they interact. It is always wise to report what happened in each layer.

You need to keep your cloud provider involved every step of the way in order to avoid any policy or legal issues that might occur due to your penetration test. This will also help you determine which approach is optimal and how it should be applied to the different applications. Most providers will have recommended procedures that will result in the most accurate results on their networks.

General Advice on Cloud Pen Testing

Another thing you should keep in mind is who is on the penetration team. If you are running this in-house, you will always have to assume that not everything has been found. Testing teams that come from within the company will usually leave some room for oversight. They know too much about the applications from the start and might always miss some things that they don't think are worth looking at. White hat hackers are the safer method, though a bit more expensive. They will search through your system more efficiently and in great detail.

Always make sure to see which practices are the most efficient with your provider, as well as which applications you will test and which requirements need to be met with the pen test. Using proven approaches is usually a good way to start.

Penetration testing is more important now than it was ever before. It is the only way to make sure that the things you have on the cloud are as secure as possible in order to accommodate for as many users as possible.

Pen testing is not an option these days. It's the only way to prove that your cloud-based applications and data are secure enough to allow the maximum amount of user access with the minimum amount of risk.

How Do On-premises Security and Cloud Security Compare?

This is a big question for many people. People often write off cloud and immediately assume that saving your data on servers inside of an office is the more secure option. This is usually the case due to the fact that you own the hardware and software when you store your data on-premises. This, however, can be detrimental due to the fact that some of the best cloud providers can give you a great deal of security that you might not get on-premises.

To be clear, the cloud system is impressive due to the fact that it is made to give 99.99 percent durability and make everything stored available all of the time. This kind of availability can not be replicated on premise due to the limitations of the hardware and software that is available to you. In order to recreate these results, it would take a huge investment and a huge number of people to manage.

Before being quick to decide which option you are going to go for you need to consider a lot of things. You need to take your budget and how big your security team is into consideration. If your answer seems to be lacking, remember that cloud providers have large teams that will deal with these things for you and have automated systems that constantly protect the system. To make a long story short, cloud companies have dedicated a large amount of time and money to make their systems what they are and it makes them much more reliable.

CHAPTER 8: MOST COMMON SECURITY TOOLS

The market for security tools is as extensive as the field itself. In order to separate the hundreds of different tools, it helps to split them up into different categories.

The first category are event managers. These tools respond to events that are happening on the networks you are monitoring. They analyze the logs on your systems in order to detect these events.

Another useful kind of tool is packet sniffers which help you decode packages while digging into the traffic in order to scan their payload. Packet sniffers are used when you go deeper into security events that are happening.

Intrusion detection and prevention systems are another useful category of tools. They might sound similar to firewalls and antiviruses, but they differ in function greatly. When it comes to this software, you should always think of them as a perimeter around your network which is there to spot any unauthorized activity.

Of course, not every tool can be classified into a category due to how specific they are when it comes to function and design. They, however, can be very useful for a lot of different situations.

It is very hard to determine which tools are better than others in different categories due to the different purposes they might have. Most of the tools that we are about to talk about are vastly different from one another and you can never say that one is definitely better than another. This means that it is hard to select tools for each different job, but here are some widely used tools that you should always take into consideration when you are going into a job.

SolarWinds Log and Event Manager

You might not have heard about SolarWinds before, but you should listen closely now. This company has made a vast amount of useful administration tools over a number of years. In the NetFlow collector and analyzer market, SolarWinds's NetFlow Traffic Analyzer is a widely-loved tool. Another great tool that SolarWinds has given us is the Network Performance Monitor, one of the best in the market for SNMP network monitoring tools. To keep it short, the thing that you should know about SolarWinds is that they offer a wide variety of free tools that you can use for different jobs and can fulfill many different roles that you might find yourself trying to fill out. Network and system administrators are often grateful to have SolarWinds, as it is a great source of useful tools.

SolarWinds Log and Event Manager Screenshot

When we are talking about SolarWinds, it is hard to ignore some of their greatest pieces of software. If you are looking for network security tools you will first want to check out the LEM, short for Log and Event Manager. This is a simple choice when you are looking for a Security and Event manager system that is very beginner friendly. This is the tool that you want to start with. In the entry-level SIEM market, it is perhaps the most competitive option. When you are dealing with SolarWinds, you can expect to get everything that any basic system would have and something more. The SolarWinds LEM coms with a great log management feature and runs on an impressive engine.

The LEM will also provide you with impressive response features. It spots threats in real-time and is very reliable at what it does. The tool works great when you are trying to protect yourself from zero-day exploits and threats that you do not know anything about due to the fact that it is not based on signature making. Behavior is what this tool is looking for. You will rarely need to update it. One of the best assets of the LEM is the dashboard. The system is very simple and makes short work of finding anomalies and reporting them.

If you are looking to buy the SolarWinds LEM you need to be ready to pay 4,585 US dollars. If you are unsure about the purchase there is always the 30-day trial that the company offers.

SolarWinds Network Configuration Manager

The LEM is not the only impressive piece of software that SolarWinds can boast. They have several other tools that are focused on network security. One of them is their Network Configuration Manager which is used to keep watch over your equipment and make sure that all of it is configured based on certain standards. What it does for your security is that it spots unauthorized changes in your system. This is useful due to the fact that these changes can be a great sign of a pending attack.

The main function of this software is that it helps you recover by restoring your system to the last configurations that were authorized. It also points out the changes and keeps the information in a configuration file. Another thing that it helps you out with is compliance. It helps you pass audits due to the standardized reports that it makes while working.

The Network Configuration Manager comes at a price of 2,895 US dollars. The price can change depending on the managed nodes that you select. This software, like the one before, comes with a 30-day trial if you are unsure about purchasing it.

SolarWinds User Device Tracker

This is another one of the amazing tools that SolarWinds offers. It is a great tool that anyone working in computer security should have. It tracks endpoint devices and users in order to improve your security. You can use it in order to identify which ports are being used and which are available.

This tool is great in situations where you are expecting an attack with a specific target. The tools helps you by pinpointing where the user that shows suspicious activity is. The searches conducted through this software are based on username, IP/MAC addresses, and hostnames. The search can go a bit deeper and go as far as scanning previous connections of the suspect.

The starting price of the User Device Tracker starts out at 1,895 US dollars. It, again, changes based on how many ports the system needs to track. Like the previous programs, this one comes with a 30-day trial as well.

Wireshark

When talking about Wireshark, it would be offensive to say that it is just a security tool. This tool is widely loved and used. It is hailed to be one of the best capture and analysis packages. This tool is used to analyze network traffic in great depth. It can capture and decode any package so that you can inspect the data they contain.

Wireshark has accumulated a great reputation. Due to the quality of service that it provides, it has pretty much become the standard for the other tools in the market. The competition always tries to emulate it as much as possible. Many administrators use the Wireshark in order to check the captures that they got through other software. This was done so commonly that the newer versions of the software will offer you the option to, upon set-up, run a capture file that you already have in order to immediately start going through traffic. Where the tool shines the most is the filters that it comes with. They are a great addition, as they help you point out the exact data that is relevant to you.

The software is hard to get used to. There are courses that run across multiple days that give instructions on using it. Despite that, it is worth learning how to use Wireshark. It is an extremely valuable tool to any administrator. The tool is free and can be used on most operating systems. You can get your own on the official website.

Nessus Professional

Among solutions for identifying malware, issues, and vulnerabilities, the Nessus Professional is one of the most used. Millions of professionals use the Nessus Professional due to the view from the outside that it provides them with. It also gives you a great deal of insight into how you can improve the security of your system.

The Nessus Professional gives one of the most broad coverages when it comes to threats. It employs a great deal of impressive intelligence and is very easy to use. The software is updated fairly often as well, which means that you will never have troubles with never-before-seen problems. It has a fairly extensive package when it comes to vulnerability scanning.

If you want to employ the services of the Nessus Professional you will have to pay 2,190 US dollars a year. If you are not sure about making the investment, you can make use of the 7-day trial.

Snort

Among open-source IDSs, Snort stands out among the best. This intrusion detection system was made in 1998. It fell into the ownership of the Cisco System in 2013. Snort entered the Open Source Hall of Fame in 2009. This means that it has been recognized as one of the greatest open source software ever. This speaks volumes.

There are three modes of operation in the snort: sniffer, packet logger, and network intrusion detection. The sniffer mode is the basic mode of operation and its main function is reading network packets and showing their contents. The packet logger is fairly similar, except for the fact that the scanned packets are logged onto the disk. The most interesting mode is the intrusion detection mode. It analyzes traffic as instructed by a ruleset that was set by you. Based on what kind of threat it found, you can go through several different lines of action.

Snort can find many different kinds of cracks in the system that can be a sign of a potential attack that can happen in the future. Snort has a website from which you can download it.

TCPdump

If you were ever interested in which packet sniffer was the first, look no further than Tcpdump. The first release of the software was in 1987. Ever since then, it has been regularly updated and maintained. However, the core of the software always stayed the same. Most Unix-like systems come with TCPdump pre-installed, as it is the standard tool for those operating systems.

The default way of functioning for the TCPdump is capturing the traffic in dumps on the screen. You might notice that this is fairly similar to the sniffer mode we talked about before. DUmps can be piped in order to capture specific files for further analysis, similar to the packer logger mode. Wireshark is usually used in tandem with TCPdump.

The greatest strength of the TCPdump is the fact that it easily captures filters and makes use of several Unix commands in order to make the work far shorter and easier. If you have a good knowledge of the Unix-like systems it will not be a problem for you to deal with traffic and capture the specific parts you are interested in.

Kismet

There is a lot to be said about Kismet. It is an intrusion detection system, packet sniffer, and network detector all in one. Its preferred function is when you are working on LAN. It works with most wireless cards and can go through many different kinds of traffic. This tool is compatible with Linux, OS X, OpenBSD, NetBSD, and FreeBSD. The Kismet has very limited support for Windows systems due to the fact that very few network adapters support Kismet's monitoring mode.

This software is licensed under the Gnu GPL License. The way that it differs from other wireless network detectors lies in the fact that the work it does is done passively. It does not make use of loggable packets, but directly detects the presence of access points. It also makes connections between them. Among open-source wireless network monitoring tools, it is the most used.

Nikto

Nikto is another piece of excellent open-source software. It is one of the most popular web server scanners. Its main function is running web servers through a huge number of tests in order to find traces of several thousands of different programs that can be threatening for your security. It can work through different versions of a lot of different servers. It checks the server configurations and checks for anomalies in the system.

Nikto is designed for speed rather than stealth. It will test a web server in the quickest time possible but its passage will show up in log files and be detected by intrusion detection and prevention systems.

Nikto is licensed under the GNU GPL. It can be downloaded from its home on GitHub.

OpenVAS

The OpenVAS, also known as the Open Vulnerability Assessment System, is a set of tools that give a great deal of extensive vulnerability scanning. Most of the components of the system are open-source and the software is completely free.

OpenVAS has two primary components. The first component of the software is the scanner. It, as the name suggests, is responsible for scanning the computers. The manager is the second component. The manager works as a controller for the scanner and works with the results of the scans. The Network Vulnerability Tests database is an additional component that you can add to the software to make it more efficient. You can download the software from two softwares: the Greenborne Security Feed and Greenborne Community Feed. The latter one is free while the first one is paid.

OSSEC

OSSEC stands for Open Source SECurity. It is a host-based program which is used for intrusion detection. This kind of detection system is different from the network-based counterparts due to the fact that the host itself runs the program. Trend Micro owns OSSEC. In the IT security field, this name has quite a bit of weight.

The primary usage of this software is in Unix-like software where its work is dedicated to scanning configuration and files. It sees some usage on Windows systems too, where it keeps an eye on the registry. The tool alerts you via the console or email whenever something suspicious is detected.

OSSEC has a relatively big drawback, just like any other host-based IDS. You have to install a new instance on every device that you are looking to protect. This is mitigated somewhat due to the fact that the information can be funneled to a centralized console.

OSSEC is also licensed under the GNU GPL. If you want to use it, you can download it from the website.

OSSEC is also distributed under the GNU GPL license and it can be downloaded from its own website.

Nexpose

Nexpose is another widely-used tool. It is made by Rapid7 and is used for managing vulnerabilities. It does all of the things a vulnerability manager can. It fulfils the so-called vulnerability manager lifecycle. This means that the software deals with all of the phases that are involved in the process.

When it comes to the features that it comes with, it is a complete whole. There are many interesting features to the software like the virtual scanning option and dynamic discovery. It can scan many different kinds of environments and can handle a number of IP addresses. It is a software in development and is constantly growing.

There are two versions of the product that you can get. There is a community edition which has way less features than the full commercial versions whose prices start at 2,000 US dollars a year. If you have any questions about the software or are looking to download Nexpose, visit the official website.

GFI LanGuard

The GFI LanGuard is hailed as an excellent IT security tool for businesses. This tool was made to help you with scanning networks and automatic patching. It also helps you meet compliance standards. This software is compatible with most operating systems.

GFI LanGuard has a very intuitive dashboard which helps out with identifying viruses as well. It works with web browsers as well. Another strength of the software is the fact that it works with a huge number of different kinds of devices.

If you are looking to purchase the GFI LanGuard, you will notice that there can be a wide variety of different options when it comes to additional features. The price is flexible and is renewed on a yearly basis. If you are not certain about purchasing the software you can try the trial version first.

Security Tools for The Cloud

As I have mentioned before, cloud has become a popular option when it comes to storing software and data due to the fact that it is a very efficient and safe method of keeping your digital valuables safe. The cloud comes with lower costs, easier scaling, and additional mobility. These prospects lead to many businesses moving their data from on-premises to cloud. This, in turn, made hackers more and more inclined to figure out new methods on attacking systems in order to be able to crack clouds. This is why many providers like Dropbox and Evernote give you many different policies that are slowly taking over the business world.

However, the cloud does have flaws of its own. There have been issues regarding data privacy and residency. These issues are, of course, not enough for people to forsake the cloud. This is why there has been a rise on the Interest of cloud-related security as users and providers are always trying to find ways to mitigate some of the risks.

If you are looking to place your business on the cloud, there are a few tools that you should always keep in mind when you want to keep your data safe. However, before talking about them you should first get to know what Shadow IT is.

The term Shadow IT accounts for any systems or services that are used on the data of the organization without the approval of the organization. Shadow IT is nothing new, but it started becoming a rising issue due to the rise of the popularity of the cloud.

This makes it harder for companies to keep their data safe due to the fact that it makes policies harder to implement.

Three out of the following five tools focus on mitigating the security risks that you might run into while dealing with cloud computing.

Bitglass

Bitglass has not been completed yet and is still in beta. It offers protection for the data of your business. Bitglass can be used on both computers and mobile devices. It aims to maintain your data's visibility and reduce the risk of that data being lost on either the device or the cloud itself.

Bitglass covers several types of security due to how much has been combined in this package. When talking about what it can do for cloud applications, Bitglass can do several things. It can detect the usage of the applications and encrypt the data that you have uploaded to the cloud.

Another great thing about Bitglass is the fact that it can track your data no matter where it is on the Internet. This means that you have vision on the data no matter where it goes and in whose hands it is. It also mitigates a great deal of risk when it comes to compromised data due to device loss. Bitglass has the ability to wipe a device of your data without having to take any additional steps.

Skyhigh Networks

Skylight Networks uses logs from firewalls and proxies that already exist in order to analyze and secure your cloud applications. It tracks the usage of the applications from both authorized and unauthorized sources.

You can customize the risk assessment in order to make sure that the results are what you want to see about your system, without any additional unnecessary information. Another great thing Skyhigh can do is detect inconsistencies in your system, as well as data leaks.

The last notable feature of the Skyhigh Networks is that it has 3-Click Security. This means that it can employ policies across the entire cloud and give you direct access to applications without using device agents or VPNs. On top of that, you can use Skyhigh to encrypt data and protect it.

Netskope

Netskope is specifically made with shadow IT in mind. It can monitor cloud apps and discover anomalies on your network. It monitors a wide variety of different activities on your network and will provide you with extensive reports on your analytics and the gathered information.

It will help you out with the questions you might have regarding business and security in order to spot out vulnerabilities in your system.

Another great feature of the Netskope is the policy enforcement that can help you keep an eye on your employees while they interact with applications on the cloud, all while stopping any activity that you might deem to be unwanted. It allows for the employee to increase their productivity, while not hurting your security.

CipherCloud

CipherCloud aims to encrypt and tokenize your data in order to secure your cloud. Unlike the previous few tools, this one does not focus on shadow IT. Rather, it makes sure to make the known parts of the cloud as secure as possible.

CipherCloud is fairly specific due to the fact that the data you upload is encrypted upon upload and decrypted while it is being downloaded. Your business network will maintain the encryption keys that are used in the process. This means that any unauthorized user will just get a batch of unreadable text instead of useful data.

CipherCloud can also detect malware and prevent loss of data. There are several builds for the CipherCloud that are specialized specifically towards helping out specific systems, while there are several that work with any application on the cloud.

Okta

Okta is quite unique among these five solutions for cloud applications. Okta's aim is to make sure that there is a secure SSO, short for Single Sign-On, for all of the applications that your business owns. Okta can interact with most commonly used applications that you might encounter in most businesses.

Okta has many useful features that you will be grateful to have like mobile device support and multifactor authentication.

The software will provide you with detailed audit logs, which means that you will be able to track the access that your users have to your cloud apps. Another great thing is the centralized control panel from which you can control the access policies across the whole system. It gives you the option of role-based administration as well.

Cloud Penetration Testing From the Point of View of the Customer

When it comes to on-premise penetration testing, you would usually assume that you will be the owner of all of the components and that any testing that you do will be done under your supervision and with your approval. In the cloud, penetration testing works a little differently. The major drawback of the cloud is the fact that consumers and providers share the responsibility when it comes to computer security. Both of these groups are eligible to do penetration testing on the applications on the cloud. There are two things that you need to think about when you are looking to do penetration testing on the cloud. The first thing that you need to consider is if you are a consumer or a provider. The other factor is the service model you have selected.

The Responsibilities of Consumers and Providers

Cloud providers have a vast variety of different opportunities when it comes to penetration testing, even the most brutal ones like DDoS testing and red team testing. There is a huge amount of competition when it comes to the cloud service market. There are many giants that provide excellent service and the need to improve is getting more and more overwhelming.

Cloud users have been more and more interested in cybersecurity. They often interact with their providers in order to get more involved in the security process and penetration testing.

The consumers themselves have a much more limited access to applications and penetration testing in the cloud. These restrictions heavily depend on the model that your cloud service provider employs.

Penetration Testing Depending on the Cloud Service Model

There are three different cloud service models: SaaS (software as a service), PaaS (platform as a service), and IaaS (infrastructure as a service). These three models are different from one another due to how responsibilities are divided between the provider and consumer when it comes to cloud layers.

In order to understand these models, you first need to get to know the eight layers of a cloud:

- **Facility (buildings).**
- **Network (both physical and virtual).**
- Computers and storage (specifically file storage and hardware supplying CPU).
- Hypervisor (The hypervisor is used in virtualized environments. The job of the hypervisor is handling the allocation of the resources between the machines in the system.).
- Operating system (OS) and Virtual machine (VM) (These two are considered to be in the same layer due to the fact that when it comes to non-virtualized environments the job of running storage hardware falls to the OS, while in virtualized environments the VM is responsible for this job.).
- Solution stack (makes use of databases and programming languages).

- Application (this layer is composed out of the applications used by the users).

- Application program interface (API) or Graphical user interface (GUI) (consumers and customers use this layer to interact with the system).

What you can do with the applications and penetration tests is directly dependent on what kind of control you have over the layers. The different kinds of models give you different extents of control over the layers.

IaaS model

The IaaS model is specific because the control over the OS and virtual machine, as well as the upper cloud levels, falls to the user. The provider is responsible for the connectivity of the hardware and network. This means that consumers are allowed to execute penetration testing on the API/GUI, application, solution stack, and the VM layers.

PaaS model

In the PaaS model, the provider gives all of the software and hardware that is necessary to run an application, while the consumer only deploys the application. This model gives the consumer fewer layers to deal with: the API/GUI and application layers to be exact.

SaaS model

The SaaS model is similar to the PaaS due to which layers can be tested by the consumer and what the provider delivers. The scope of testing is limited to the API/GUI layer. However, some providers that employ this model let their users run their own applications independent of the system. These applications can be tested by the consumer whenever they want.

Things You Should Remember as a Cloud Penetration Testing Customer

There are two golden rules when it comes to penetration testing on the cloud:

- Always ask your provider if you want to run a test
- Run penetration tests only on the layers that you control

Most providers have certain requirements that need to be fulfilled before they allow you to get into their systems. Usually, you can find this information on the website of the provider. If you make any unauthorized penetration test or do testing without meeting the requirements, your account will be shut down because the provider needs to take care of the security of the other users as well so they can not take any risks with suspicious activity.

A provider's job is not an easy one. They always have so many things to think about and balance out. They always have to make sure that the data of their customers is safe, but still leave the interests of the customer unharmed due to the security policies the provider might implement. The provider is not all-powerful, so the penetration testing that they can do must be done within their own domain. It's a good thing that no cloud provider will access your data without your permission, so you can rest easy knowing that your privacy is safe.

CHAPTER 9: WHAT DO I NEED TO KNOW

How do you get a job? What education and experience do you need?

To say that ethical hacking is a job like any other would be highly incorrect. It does not require any kind of diploma or certification. Knowledge and experience are all that matters in this line of work. No matter how many diplomas you have, the most important thing is your resourcefulness and know-how. The certificates can be easy to acquire once you prove yourself.

Do you need any certifications or licenses?

In order to be an ethical hacker, you will not have to have any certificates. It is, however, nice to have them, as they are confirmation of your skill in the field. There are many different certifications whose value depends on the job that you are aiming for. You should do your research when you are aiming for a certification. The most valuable skills you can have in this field of work, other than the knowledge itself, are persistence, communication skills and problem solving.

The Nature of the Work

What lies behind the surface level of the job? What will you be doing most of the time?

If you are doing this line of work, you will get access to some very vulnerable systems. Once you are inside of them, you will notice just how much damage a well-placed attack could do to the system and the corporation itself. You will see the connections they shouldn't have, programs that need patching, if the software and hardware are properly used, and if the passwords stored on the system are safe. Every network is just a mass of interconnected systems that are easier to crack into than it might appear at first. This is especially important with networks that take care of your money or personal information. An important thing that you need to keep in mind is how informed you are. Social networks are a great place to find out some fresh news before it pops up in other mediums.

Most of the time while doing this line of work will be spent on just probing around networks and poking away at potential vulnerabilities and documenting the findings and informing your clients about them. At times you might feel like you are back in school due to the sheer amount of reports that you will make as a hacker. The reports need to be informative and concise, as they are the only insight that your client will have into their systems.

It is important for the client to be involved every step of the way. Even though the process is very open, the client might get lost in all of the little intricacies of the process due to the technical knowledge needed to understand them.

What are the common assumptions that people make about the line of work?

People often connect the word "hacker" with malicious acting people that deal in illegal activities. This, however, as I have said many times, is untrue. Hackers are people that like to explore how new tools and software can be used in order to solve problems and open up new lanes of attacking. The malicious individuals that use their knowledge to hurt people or steal money and information are not hackers. These individuals are mere criminals and nothing more. The hacking community resents the fact that they need to identify as "ethical hackers" due to what kind of reputation the criminals gave the word. The term "cracker" was always a possibility when talking about criminal hackers, but is often overlooked.

Some people like to look at the hacking process and think of it as if it were a magician's performance. On the contrary, hacking is a well devised process that is aimed towards systematically going through a system in order to improve a network or a system. Despite what some people think, hackers are nothing other than people who have great insight into how systems works. Computers will always do only what they are told and nothing else.

Another wrong assumption people like to make is that every test a white hat runs is the same. Sadly, this field of work is barely explored and penetration testing is fairly unknown to most individuals as a term. There are many different penetration tests that all have a different skill requirement.

How many hours a day are you going to work?

The amount of time you will require to spend daily while working heavily depends on what kind of activity you are partaking in. If a high-end company hired you to run a penetration test, you will have to work 8-10 hours a day. Every job can take up to 10 weeks to complete. If you are just looking around the system or network for vulnerabilities, the amount of time you are going to spend on it depends on you.

If you are called by a company in order to help them recover from a security breach, then your hours might go through the roof. All-nighters are nothing strange for people in this line of work. Stopping an attack from further damaging the system is not an easy task, especially due to the fact that it is your responsibility to control the damage and help the company get back into action.

Are there any tips and shortcuts that can help you out in the job?

Make sure to always keep up with the news. There are always new methods popping up and you might find someone who found an easier way to do something you are interested in. Always keep a documentation of your exploits and the information you gathered in order to keep track of what you have been doing. By doing this you can avoid making yourself feel bad over wasting time or not seeing the solution in time.

Always remember that there is no such thing as too much communication. No hacker has ever been fired due to giving a client too much info about the system. You will rarely find a client that will instruct you to give them less information. Generally, clients like to be informed on what is happening on their system no matter how miniscule it is, and they will usually appreciate the work you put into relaying that information in an understandable fashion.

Are there any things you can do to stand out from the rest of the white hats?

There is a common misconception among companies that an ethical hacker's job is to just scan the system in order to find a vulnerability and that there is nothing more to it. This, however, isn't true. A white hat hacker's job is far more extensive and in-depth. They will always try to figure out why the program is vulnerable and how that vulnerability can be abused by a malicious individual, as well as the actual amount of damage that a successful black hat hacker can cause.

Finding vulnerabilities in a network is fairly easy. The main chunk of work that a hacker needs to do comes from analyzing what the vulnerability means for the system. You might want to know what the hacker could do and would want to do by using that vulnerability, as well as how the vulnerability interferes with other parts of the system. It can also help you figure out how a criminal hacker would go about cracking into the system, preventing any kind of similar attack from being effective.

What about the job is the worst part and how can you deal with things like that?

Few things can throw you off like specific clients. You might sometimes be hired by people who are not really interested in what is going on in their system and are just looking to do it for the sake of doing it. Another kind of client that will cause some substantial stress is the indifferent kind. Some companies are not always happy to hire a white hat hacker to help them out due to the fact that they think that repairing the damage left by the hacker will always be much cheaper than hiring a professional to help them improve the security of their networks. On the other hand, the more unwilling clients might hire a white hat hacker purely out of fear about their system being cracked. This can be compared to when your car starts making weird noises. You will go see a mechanic as soon as possible in order to see if something is wrong.

Some customers might be concerned that the services of a white hat hacker can cost a pretty penny. This is not always the only concern, as people who look for services are often people who rely on their IT skills as a job. If you detect a lot of vulnerabilities and problems, you might make the individual look bad.

The best thing you can do in situations like this is to just keep up the good work. Always do your best and make sure to report everything that you find, as well as what that could mean for the network. Remember, you are not responsible for protecting the system yourself. That responsibility falls on the client himself. The best you can do is hope that they will do right by themselves.

Where is the enjoyment in the job? What makes it so attractive?

It is hard to pinpoint exactly what the best thing about the job is. Some people take great satisfaction in the fact that they are doing something that would be illegal if the situation were any different. People often joke about how they start to think like a criminal after a while. This is true in most cases and can be a fun way to approach the job.

There are many interesting people in the sector. You will always have fun exchanging knowledge and stories from work with them, as well as potentially make new friends.

What might give you the most satisfaction in the job, however, is the fact that you are making a huge impact on someone's life. You are helping them not only feel more secure, but also be more secure. You are influencing someone's life in a very good way and it can be quite rewarding on its own. To be honest, the pay is pretty good, too.

Is there anything that you would like your clients to know before looking for your help?

There are several things that clients should often keep in mind. The first, and perhaps the most important thing you should remember about white hat hackers is the fact that they are not superheroes. They are not capable of solving all of your problems just by swooping in. Sometimes clients like to think that once you get into their system you will make it completely safe and that they can run carefree. This, however, is wishful thinking.

While many white hat hackers would like it to work that way, the reality is a bit harder to swallow. It is important for every client to be realistic. It is up to them to decide which parts of the system are the most important and what kinds of risks are acceptable when it comes to protecting them. It is impossible to make a completely impenetrable system. There is always that one vulnerability that you can't see or a new technique that you could not have possibly accounted for. What this means is that a white hat hacker's job is not done when they find a way to prevent a potential attack. They always need to assess the situation in order to see what can be done in order to prevent some successful attack from getting out of hand.

Nobody can protect themselves from a threat that they do not know exists. This is why there are a few steps that you can take to help out the hacker you hired to make sure that they have done everything that was possible to keep your system safe. Before a hacker does a penetration test, you should always provide them with as much important information on the system as possible.

The penetration test aims to find a part of your system that is vulnerable to attacks and use it to show how much that could impact the system itself. Nobody likes their money gone or their sensitive personal information missing, so you should always act quickly to fix the vulnerability as soon as the hacker discovers it.

Something that all clients should know is that the penetration testing is the easy part. Learning from your mistakes and conducting your business in safer ways is the difficult part.

How much can you make while doing this job?

Well, the first thing to point out is that your expectations will be met most of the time as long as they are reasonable. The second thing that is worth mentioning is that hacking is similar to other lines of work when it comes to how much hard work is rewarded. If you work hard enough and get good enough, you will make quite a pretty penny. If you are looking to start working for a large amount of money immediately after you got a certification or gained extensive knowledge in the field, you are going to work yourself to a pulp. Companies can be quite ruthless when it comes to the amount of work they place on you. You might be forced to travel a lot and work long hours. Some hackers often say that, at this point, sleep is a luxury. If you are aiming to have a substantial amount of money flowing into your pocket while working in a healthy manner, you might have to accumulate years of experience in IT fields and computer security.

How does one advance in this field?

Well, this question is an interesting one. It usually depends on the individual that we are talking about. You will gain new knowledge on a daily basis no matter which key area you work in. While these skills are usually different from one line of work to another, gaining experience is the key to progressing. While doing well on exams and getting fancy certificates might help you out, the most important thing you can have is skill while working.

There is another way to stand out among the people you work with. There are conferences held on a yearly basis. If you conduct interesting research and prove it to be useful, your name might start getting a bit of weight to throw around. The more you involve yourself in these conferences, the higher the chance of your name getting mentioned is.

What do clients tend to overvalue or undervalue?

In most cases, clients do not see how valuable they themselves are to the process itself. They like to think that a good hacker is all you need to keep the bad people away. This, however, is untrue, as the client needs to do most of the work when it comes to keeping himself or herself safe. People are also prone to making excuses as to why they are never going to be hacked. They like to say that their firm is too small or that they have no valuable information that someone might want. This all changes fairly quickly once their systems actually do get hacked.

Another common mistake companies make is when they compare themselves to other companies. Some boardroom talks tend to fall down to this. They feel as if they are wasting money if they spent more on security than another similar company.

What people often overvalue, however are compliance standards. People like to think that if you meet these standards, your system is completely safe and nothing wrong can happen when a hacker tries to get into it. What you need to understand about compliance standards is that they are not representative of the performance needed to keep your system secure. They are a rough outline of the absolute minimum in order to not be fined. In order to truly be safe, you will need to go leagues and miles beyond what the compliance standards dictate.

What is the most important thing to remember?

You need to put your heart and soul into it. This is a market that just keeps growing and it is hungry for individuals that are interested in playing around with systems and seeing what makes them tick and how to keep them ticking on.

Make sure to enjoy the process of learning. If it looks like a drag to learn the skills you already know over and over again, then some of the less glamorous parts of the job will surely bore you. You should never stop hoping, though. It is easy to find some specific kind of job that is fun for you and makes you feel fulfilled.

Conclusion

White hat hacking is not something new. In fact, it has been here for a long time, just under different names or under no name at all. There has been a great deal of controversy surrounding white hat hacking for a very long time. Ever since cybercrime started being a common practice among criminals, the word "hacker" has been steadily gaining a malicious reputation. Due to how far computer technology has evolved over a relatively short period of time, it is natural for information to be moved from a physical form to a digital form. There are many criminal organizations that value information over anything so it is natural for them to always find new ways to invade systems. This means that it is more important than ever to have secure systems. Valuable data like passwords that we use every day are something very valuable and that we need to protect.

White hat hacking came as a not-so-obvious solution to finding new ways to protect our systems. Think of a system as if it was a human being. When a person gets sick their body gets weaker and they suffer some damage. However, long-term, if the body gets through the disease, it will get more resilient to the disease in the future. The same can be said for injuries. If you break a bone in one place multiple times over a period of time, the new tissue that will replace the damage will be more resilient than ever before. White hat hacking works on a similar principle. In order to make sure that your system is secure you need to pad out as many vulnerabilities as possible. It is hard to tell where these vulnerabilities are if they are not exploited. However, you can't really wait for an attack to happen in order to spot the vulnerability and hope for the best. Once a malicious hacker gets into your system, there is no telling how far they will go or what they will do. Still, it was necessary to have a method that would help organizations keep their systems up to date with the most recent hacking tools and techniques in order to create countermeasures.

White hat hacking is the only real way to do this. To make the system less vulnerable to a hacker attack is to expose it to danger. This is not something you would trust anyone to do, as it is an extremely precise and delicate process. The professionals you hire to do this for you have to be meticulous in their work and have extensive knowledge of computers.

The problem with being a white hat hacker is that many people automatically make a correlation between you and malicious individuals that do the same activities as you but for different reasons. The calling of hacker is not considered a bad thing everywhere though. People in the IT sector have great respect for certified white hat hackers as it means that they are people that have a huge amount of knowledge in the field and that they use that knowledge to do good for other people. The people who look at white hats as if they are criminals usually do not know what white hats actually do and just focus on the hacker part of the title. This is mainly why white hats do not flaunt the calling and prefer to keep it off of their CVs.

White hat hackers are, however, a force for good. They use the same methods as crackers but do so with the permission of the owner of the system they are hacking into and do so in order to improve the security of the system. The point is that they are the polar opposite of black hat hackers as they make their jobs much more difficult.

The field of white hat hacking has been growing rapidly. This is in great part due to how much cybercrimes have grown over the past several decades, so there are always companies that are looking to hire a good white hat hacker. They are ready to pay a large amount of money but will drain you of your time and energy as it is more than a full-time job. Luckily, freelancing as a white hat hacker is always an option. This road is a bit slower but will take you to more favorable results. As I have mentioned before, the job only requires knowledge and experience, so working hard is the key to success. If you manage to prove yourself in the field, you will rarely have your hands free. You can get several certificates to prove your expertise in the field, but, again, this is not necessary as all you need to do to get a good job is to prove yourself to the employer. After that, it is smooth sailing.

The job might not be for everyone, however. At times, you might be stuck doing the same thing over and over again over a prolonged period of time and that is just not interesting to some people. On the other hand, you will find the line of work extremely interesting if you like learning new things, as new methods are discovered all the time. The job takes a great amount of flexibility, as nothing you do will exactly be done by the textbook. Most of the time you will just be thinking as a cracker in order to get into the system, but before that, there is a phase where you must meticulously gather data on the system. The fun part starts when you actually get to dig into the system. You will poke around to find some weaknesses and then follow a hacking plan in order to determine what kind of damage a malicious user could do from that point. During all of this, you will have to do the thing that so many people dread: making reports.

Reports are the most important result of penetration testing, as they are the direct connection between the employer and the hacker. The reports give a run-down on what the vulnerabilities are, how they can be exploited, and how they can be fixed. A client needs this information in order to determine what needs to be done down the line to ensure that the vulnerability will never be exploited by a malicious individual.

Being a relatively new field, hacking has great promise for creators and explorers. People who are the most renowned in the community are people who develop tools and methods that white hat hackers can use to be more efficient at what they do. Making one of these tools takes a large amount of money and time, so this is a job for only the bravest and the most skilled.

Always remember that, no matter what the media tells you, not all hackers are evil. There are those who use their technical knowledge to take advantage of other people for their own benefit, but white hat efforts are dedicated to stopping this. There are many skilled individuals in the line of work whose names themselves speak volumes.

In this day and age, white-hat hacking has become a necessity if you want your systems to stay safe. Hiring a white hat hacker might put you back a pretty penny at times, but it is well worth it if you have any sensitive or classified data that you don't want to be stolen or destroyed.

Some people underestimate the importance of computer security, saying things like: "It won't happen to me because I do not have any useful data," or "The chances are too low." These people realize the mistake when it's too late and they have already been hacked. You should always stay on top of your computer security, as you never know what could happen and when you can be attacked.

Always remember to stay safe while doing anything with your system. Your data might not be valuable to a hacker, but it is valuable to you and you should not let it be lost.

www.ingramcontent.com/pod-product-compliance
Lightning Source LLC
LaVergne TN
LVHW022309200926
848481LV00004B/1250